THE ULTIMATE PERSONAL FINANCE GUIDE FOR TEENS

LEARN THE SECRETS OF MONEY MANAGEMENT TO
BECOME WEALTHY AND LIVE A STRESS-FREE LIFE

CARLOS A. DAVILA

TABLE OF CONTENTS

INTRODUCTION

"You have to have a never ending thirst for learning."

— MR. BEAST

The beep of your alarm wakes you up. You look at the watch, and it's 6:30 a.m. Good... There's still enough time before Mom knocks on your door and asks you to get ready for school. So you do the most natural thing that you can do—unlock your phone and open Instagram. Nothing like starting a day with a good old dose of social media, right? (Not really, but we do it anyway!) As you scroll through your feed, you see your classmate Kate's post. She went on a vacation with her parents to Bali this summer, and that's all she's been posting about. Every day, there's a new picture of the blue ocean and Kate posing in a weird-looking colorful beach dress that invariably has umbrella prints. We get it; you went to Bali, and you are rich. How long are you going to show that off? Moving on to viewing stories. There's David lifting weights at the gym, a couple of dog and cat accounts you follow, and then there's Paul playing basketball and wearing those limited-edition basketball shoes. Now, you're not a player or anything, but those shoes are giving unmissable "cool person" vibes, and that is not something that should be compromised on.

There's no point in lying to yourself; you've been wanting to buy a nice pair of sports shoes for a while now, and Paul's Instagram story acted as the final push. You opened your favorite shopping website, looked for a similar pair, and voila! Order placed. You feel a moment of immense excitement as you check out the delivery date and other order details. But unfortunately, coupled with that excitement, there's that dreaded feeling of buyer's remorse. Thoughts like "Did I do the right thing by spending so much money?" "What will Mom and Dad say?" "Did I really need those shoes?" And "Should I cancel the order?" flood your mind, and you are soon not able to enjoy the thrill that came with buying your favorite pair of shoes. Every decision you make comes with automatic second-guessing and anxiety, so it is not a one-time occurrence. You'd definitely not like to feel this way every time you buy something or make a financial decision, but the important question is: how? By achieving financial literacy, that's how!

You're not really a child anymore, right? Your parents treat you like adults most of the time, and you are expected to know your way around the world. While that is quite achievable for the most part, making financial decisions seems to be an aspect where things don't quite go your way. And I'm not just talking about the feeling of guilt after buying something nice. How would you like to actually feel confident about money and finances? Imagine a scenario where your monthly allowance allows you to buy the things you want, save, and even get into the so-called intimidating world of investing. It sounds too good to be true but trust me, it's easier than you can imagine! It just needs a little bit of directed effort and consistency. And guess what? Your journey toward that life starts right here with this book. Please stick around and check out what it has to offer.

WHY IS FINANCIAL LITERACY NEEDED?

Take a moment to list all the subjects you are studying or have studied in high school. There's Math, Science, English, History, Art, and a bunch of others, but is money management one of them? Probably not. The biggest reason why financial literacy is a huge problem in the United States is because there are no active efforts on the part of the education system to make young people aware of these concepts. Money management isn't taught in most schools. Sure, you might have had an occasional seminar where someone from a bank would come and lead a 1-hour session on writing checks and banking practices, but that's about it. And we all know how effective *those* rare sessions can be. Most students find these to be a bother, cannot wait for them to be over, and get on with their lives.

To make matters worse, money is a sensitive topic in most homes, too. Parents don't like talking about finances in front of their kids because the general notion is that "children don't need to hear all that." I a n not challenging anyone's beliefs, but think about it for a second. I you are not taught about money, can you really expect to know he w to manage it all of a sudden? This is exactly what happens to most kids as they step into adulthood. They grow up in complete financial ignorance and then mess up once they have to manage their money. This is the story of the majority of American youth. According to the data published by United Way NCA (2023), young Americans owe over $1 trillion, and over 70% of millennials live paycheck to paycheck. This is a clear indication of the dire situation of financial literacy in the country. But you have the choice to be the exception to these statistics.

Money and financial management are both simple and complex at the same time. Let me explain why I say that. We have come a long way from the ancient barter system and metal coins. Money is now plastic and digital and can be accessed from our phones. The ease of access has opened many new doors for economic and financial development, but it has also made things complex and, at times, overwhelming. There are apps for saving, investing, budgeting, and managing your money. Everything is connected to all your devices, and you are constantly receiving notifications for every dollar you spend. Sure, it's convenient, but only when you know how to stay on top of everything. Otherwise, it's just another notification that you clear at the end of the day, along with a hundred other useless ones.

Not being aware of your finances can wreak havoc in your life, but at the same time, managing your finances efficiently can help you enjoy everything with confidence. Don't you believe that you deserve to live a comfortable life free from constant financial anxiety? I think you know the answer better than I do.

But here's a hard pill to swallow—achieving financial independence is easier said than done, which is why so many people struggle with it. I am not going to sugarcoat anything for you because you deserve to know the whole truth just the way it is. But let me also tell you this: Understanding money and related concepts isn't simple, but you can easily get into the habit if you stay committed and consistent. This is not a chapter in your syllabus, but a learning process that you'll continue for the rest of your life. Will it be worth it? Well, that's for you to find out! But I'd say having a positive financial outlook, not second-guessing yourself, and being able to manage your money independently is worth a lot. Apart from all the material things you can buy with money, financial independence will also give you two invaluable things: happiness and peace of mind.

NOW IS THE TIME TO TAKE ACTION

The most common notion that most teens have is that "I have plenty of time to think about all this stuff." True, you do have a lot of time, but my point is, why should that stop you from taking action today? Think about it this way: Managing your finances isn't a compulsory school assignment. It is something that you are doing for yourself and will help you tremendously in the future. I know it sounds a bit like a trick to get you to do your homework, but trust me, once you are done reading this book, you'll be looking at your finances from a whole new angle.

This book is a comprehensive guide that covers concepts like investing and budgeting and helps you create financial plans tailored to your needs. I understand that money can be a sensitive issue, especially when there is still so much confusion and intimidation surrounding it. With the help of this book, you'll be able to critically evaluate your financial decisions, avoid mistakes resulting from peer pressure, and build a better relationship with money so you can become rich—both in terms of money and experience! Your young age should not prevent you from becoming a wise person, and that is exactly what we will be achieving through this book. So buckle up and get ready for the financial joyride of your life! Your outlook is about to change, and you'll soon be in a position to make financial decisions much more confidently. Happy reading!

1

MONEY MYTHS BUSTED

"When writing the story of your life, don't let anyone else hold the pen."

— DRAKE

As children, we have all had our share of strange beliefs and things we felt were absolutely true. Later, as we grow up, we realize the actual truth behind some of these things, while others continue to remain an enigma. Let me tell you a few of mine and how those changed over time. When I was around five, my elder brother made me believe that every time I did something naughty, a gnome would come and take a tooth away. It was a very convenient lie because I was at the age when I was losing all my teeth. Thankfully, when they started growing again, I realized the gnomes had nothing to do with it. Another one of these started after I met my Uncle Tim when I was nine. Uncle Tim was a businessperson, and I had vaguely heard from my mom and some other family members that he had a lot of debt. Someone said this as a note of caution: "If you have a lot of debt, then you might go to jail," and it is something that stuck with me. There is a good chance that you and your family feel a little intimidated by debt if your family is not extremely wealthy. This myth was something I believed for the longest time until I figured out that there was no way one could go to jail for simply having a lot of debt as long as they were managing it properly. Think about it: All the large corporations and Fortune 500 companies take on debt worth millions of dollars to run their businesses, but are they all going to jail for that? Of course not!

Now, when I look back at that age, I often feel a bit silly for having believed these myths. But then again, the problem does not lie with me or you. According to the statistics published by the National Endowment for Financial Education (2017), one out of five American teens lacks basic financial literacy skills. So, the issue is a lot bigger than we can imagine, which is why, in this chapter, we are going to debunk some of these common myths that prevent us from learning more about our finances.

COMMON MISCONCEPTIONS ABOUT PERSONAL FINANCE FOR TEENS

I don't need to tell you how much our perceptions can shape our actions because you probably already have those instances yourself. In our teenage years, we are more susceptible to building opinions based on how we feel about things. It's just how our minds work when we are young, and let me tell you, that is a wonderful thing. To be able to feel things intensely and act on them is beautiful because emotions make us human. But unfortunately, it comes with a flipside. You can get easily influenced and have strange misconceptions, especially about things you don't know much about.

We have already established that, as adults, we could do a better job teaching teens about money. So, it is pretty obvious that most kids have a ton of misconceptions about financial aspects, similar to the ones I had when I was younger. Although there can be different types of misapprehension, here are a few common myths that young people have about money that end up causing a lot of harm to them.

I Can Save What Is Left Over at the End of the Month

This is one of the biggest misconceptions that young people have. You should never save what is left but rather fix a savings rate first and then plan your expenses accordingly. This is because if you only save the money you have left, you might not be able to save at all for some months. It is normal for us to spend a little extra sometimes, but that does not mean you should compromise your savings. Make saving money a priority, and managing your finances will become easier than ever.

College Cannot Be Afforded

It is not a secret that a college education is becoming more and more expensive with each passing day. However, that does not mean it has to be completely unaffordable. There are various kinds of financial aid available for students, and you can even take up a part-time job while you are studying to pay for your education. Skipping college without even trying to get help might not be the best idea in the long run. Sure, you can definitely get a job right after high school and start earning money but think about it in terms of skill and technical knowledge. Ten years down the line, a college graduate might get a preference for a job that you are eyeing because they have a formal degree. While you might gain experience from a job right now, you should still consider attending college because it is going to increase your professional exposure to a great extent. Getting financial assistance is easier than you think, and that is why you should not let this misconception get in the way of your higher education.

Debt Can Never Be Good

There are a lot of misconceptions surrounding debt, and most of them are very negative. Debt is always considered to be inherently bad, and owing money is almost synonymous with being in huge trouble. But that is really not the case, especially if you are managing the debts efficiently.

In this context, it is important to understand the difference between good and bad debt. Yes, you read that right! There is something called good debt, too. Any debt that will help you earn a good return in the future can be regarded as a good debt. Let's understand this with the help of an example. Suppose you are a very bright student but don't have the financial means to afford a college education all on your own. If you want to pursue higher education, you'll need to take out an educational loan. In this case, even if you are taking out a loan, it is a form of good debt because it will help you significantly improve your future earning potential. The money you are spending on education now will help you get a high-paying job, or your knowledge might pave the way for you to start your entrepreneurial venture. Good debt is any form of debt that will help you in future-proofing your current goals.

On the other hand, bad debts are those loans that are taken out to buy things that do not contribute to your long-term well-being. For instance, if you are borrowing money to buy consumer goods or spending a lot on credit cards, then it is bad debt. Once you understand the difference between good and bad debt, you will be able to manage your money better.

Budgets Are Not Needed at the Moment

For the longest time, I felt that I didn't need to budget because I was a cautious spender. To tell you the truth, in my teenage years, I did not even know how budgeting worked. Even though we have moved a generation forward, most teens today also don't know how to budget, or don't feel the need to use it in their daily lives. Irrespective of the type of spender you are and the amount of money you are making, you should make budgeting a habit because it gives you more control over your finances. When you create a budget, you get a clear picture of where you are spending your money and how you can plan better. Contrary to another popular myth, budgets are neither restrictive nor do they stop you from enjoying life. They will help you achieve your financial goals faster without having to compromise on your favorite things.

Credit Cards Are Inherently Bad

I know, I know. Just a couple of paragraphs before, I said that buying a lot of things on your credit card is bad. But hear me out. The concept of credit cards is not inherently evil as long as you pay your dues on time every month. Before we delve deeper into debunking this myth, let's quickly understand the basic principle behind credit cards. When you get a credit card, you receive something called a revolving line of credit. You are allowed a certain dollar limit called the credit limit, up to which you can spend on the card, and at the end of the month, the credit card company will send you a bill for the amount you spent. There will be a due date, and you are in the clear as long as you repay the whole amount by that date.

Suppose you have a credit limit of $2,000; as you keep spending money on the card, the limit gets reduced. Once you repay the bill, the limit is restored to the original $2,000. If you keep repaying the whole amount every month, you will be able to build a good credit score, which is beneficial when you are trying to take out a big loan for a car or a mortgage.

But let's talk a bit about why credit cards have a negative reputation, which contributes to the myth we are discussing here. Suppose you spent $700 in a particular month. When the credit card company sends you the bill, they will include not only the total amount you've spent but also something called the minimum amount due. This amount is significantly lower than what you actually spent, which is an attractive option for people with a bit of a cash crunch. Suppose the minimum amount due comes to $75 for you, which means that despite spending $700, you can get away with paying only $75. It seems too good to be true, doesn't it? That's because it is. The unpaid amount is carried forward to the next month, and the credit card company charges a very high-interest rate. Suppose you keep making minimum payments for a few months. In that case, you might soon owe more than you actually spent because of the high-interest rates, and it might take you a very long period of time to pay it back.

As long as you understand the real reason behind these myths, you will be in a position to rationally evaluate the situation. The first step toward achieving financial freedom is differentiating between misconceptions and actual facts and making decisions based on logic. Good job on taking one step in that direction.

"TOO YOUNG FOR FINANCE?" THINK AGAIN

During a family gathering last Thanksgiving, I met my 21-year-old niece after a long time. She's in college now and has a part-time job, too. I was chatting with her, and I casually asked her about how she managed her finances. She mentioned using an app for budgeting, which quite obviously made me very happy. I was getting the impression that her levels of financial literacy might be better than those of the average American young adult. So then I asked her if she had started saving or investing any money, and her response sank my heart. She said, "What for? Why do I need to invest money?" I told her that it would allow her to grow the money and even build a fund for retirement. "Retirement? I am just 21; nobody is thinking about that stuff at my age! It sounds more like a 'you' thing, Uncle, haha!" This was followed by some awkward smiles, and then both of us decided it was better to concentrate on the turkey instead of dragging this conversation out any further.

Teens and young adults tend to think that they can never be good at money matters because it's an adult thing. Of course, adults have more experience, and most of the time, they know better when it comes to financial things. But you can still achieve financial success or manage your money successfully at a young age. We live in an era of technology where information about everything is easily available. You can take your phone out and Google literally anything under the sun. Being young should definitely not stop you from learning more about so-called adult things. When I was a teenager, it was pretty hard to understand things like budgets and investments if you were not getting a degree in finance. Knowledge was not easily accessible, which made things even more complex and intimidating.

But things have changed drastically now, and the success of many very young entrepreneurs is testimony to that fact. Take the example of Alina Morse, who is the CEO and founder of Zolli Candy. A bank teller offering lollipops inspired Alina, who was only seven years old at the time, to develop lollipops that are actually healthy for your teeth (The Startup Squad, 2021). She created Zollipops, which are 100% naturally sweetened and vegan lollipops. Since then, she has expanded her candy base to include taffy, gummies, and even caramels. The highlight of all these candies is that they are tooth-friendly. Zolli Candy is now a multi-million-dollar company. Alina's unique business idea has rapidly expanded into a very successful company.

I am not asking you to compare yourself to Alina or any other young entrepreneur but to draw inspiration from their example. It is easier than you think as long as you believe in your abilities and stay committed to your efforts.

ADDRESSING THE "I'M NOT GOOD WITH NUMBERS" CONUNDRUM

Even if teens are convinced that they can learn financial management from a young age, one thing that often stops them is the belief that they have to be good with numbers. In fact, this is something that prevents a lot of adults from managing their money effectively. While there are some numbers and calculations, you don't have to do them yourself. Think about it: There are apps that split the bill between a specified number of people and inform you how much each person owes. There are online calculators that tell you how much you will be earning if you invest a specific amount for a set number of years at a given interest rate. Apps like YNAB, Goodbudget, and PocketGuard connect all your bank accounts and help you prepare a whole budget while putting in minimal effort. To put it simply, you don't have to physically calculate anything. But interestingly, if you take a keen interest in financial management in your teens, your ability to deal with numbers will improve significantly as you grow older.

Contrary to popular belief, personal finance has little to do with numbers and mathematics. The core values of money management are rooted in understanding simple concepts and building good habits. You can always use online tools and apps to help with the math part. Still, your focus should be on changing your outlook and creating a positive association with money. Here are a few important habits that you should consider building that will help you in your personal finance journey:

- Setting financial goals is an essential part of evaluating your priorities. But simply setting a bunch of goals won't do the trick. You'll need to write them down and keep them in front of you so you can remind yourself of what you're working for. A goal in your mind is just an idea, but when you write it down, you are taking an actionable step toward making it a reality.
- Make it a habit to start saving beginning in your teens. It doesn't matter if you don't have an income yet. You can save a little bit from your monthly allowance, but make sure to set a rate and do it consistently. For example, if you receive $200 per month as an allowance, save around 20% of that every month. Staying consistent will help you build a habit very quickly.
- Budgeting can seem like an intimidating activity when you are doing it for the first time. This is more true if you use a manual spreadsheet or pen and paper to create and maintain the budget. That is why it is a good idea to use a budgeting app like YNAB, Goodbudget, Everydollar, or PocketGuard. These apps will help you sync all your bank accounts and divide expenses according to specified categories. When you use apps, the whole budgeting process becomes much simpler and even more fun. Since

you're already used to using multiple apps in a day, one extra won't make much of a difference, and you'll feel more comfortable dealing with the whole process.

- You won't be able to avoid debt all your life, and the sooner you make peace with that truth, the smoother your financial journey will become. When you do end up having some debt, make sure you are trying to repay the high-interest accounts first. High-interest debt can have a cascading effect on your finances, so you should aim to get rid of it as soon as you can.
- Denial isn't going to take you anywhere, especially when it comes to your finances. For the longest time, I would often ignore the "Your account has been debited" messages because it would just make me anxious. But I wasn't doing myself a favor because, unless I checked my accounts regularly, there was no way for me to be aware of my financial situation. Staying on top of your account balances, debts, and other details will help you feel more confident about money.
- If you get a sudden impulse to buy something, take a step back and sleep on it. After 24 hours, if you still feel like you need to buy it, then go ahead and make the purchase. But interestingly, you will find that you are buying only a few things after giving it some thought. Impulse buys can be fun sometimes, but making it a habit can wreak havoc on your finances.

A big part of building good financial habits and improving your money skills is staying updated about what is going on. You can look for finance podcasts, follow finance enthusiasts on social media, and look for learning material on relevant monetary topics to ignite your interest.

INTERACTIVE ELEMENT

Okay, so we have busted some myths in this chapter, and now it is time to see how strong your myth radar has become. Let's play a fun game of two truths and one lie. I'll give you a few sets of three statements; two of them will be true, and one will be a lie. You'll need to guess the lie and see if you were thinking along the right lines. Ready?

Statement Set A

1. Budgeting helps you understand your financial position.
2. Budgeting is just a process of keeping track of how much you are spending.
3. Budgeting lists your sources of income and expenses for each month.

Statement Set B

1. You can start investing right from your teens.
2. Investments take place through apps and digital means.
3. You need quite a lot of money to start investing.

Statement Set C

1. Retirement savings should only be started once you graduate and have a well-paying job.
2. Retirement funds grow better when you have been saving for a long time due to the benefit of compounding.
3. Early planning can help you navigate potential financial difficulties once you have retired and don't have a job anymore.

Statement Set D

1. You should fix a savings rate for yourself so you can consistently save money every month.
2. Cutting back on small expenses is the best way to save a ton of money.
3. Savings can be made automatic, so you don't have to think about it every month.

Answer Key

Statement Set	Lie	Reasoning
A	2	Budgeting is much more than a simple process to keep track of your spending. It can help you identify your spending patterns and achieve financial goals faster through thorough planning.
B	3	You absolutely don't need a lot of money to start investing. In fact, you can start with as little as $50 and invest through a good app like Robinhood, Acorns, or Betterment.
C	1	You can start saving for retirement right away when you receive an allowance. There is absolutely no need to wait until you have a well-paying job to build a retirement fund.
D	2	While cutting back on small expenses can be an effective way to save a few bucks, it won't take you very far in your journey toward achieving financial freedom. Suppose you start cutting back on your Starbucks orders that you indulge in three times a week. This will help you save around $15 per week and $60 a month. But simply doing this will not help you achieve your big financial goals, and you'll need to have a more structured approach based on your needs.

Clearing the air surrounding financial myths is a very important first step toward understanding your finances and building a positive relationship with money. Now that you have done that, you're ready to delve deeper into the core financial concepts and discover the benefits they can offer. In the next chapter, we will discuss the value of money and the freedom it can represent once you understand its true meaning.

2

UNDERSTANDING THE VALUE OF MONEY

"In the simplest terms, inflation occurs when there is too much money in the system."

— ROBERT KIYOSKI

As a child, I would often hear my parents talking about the value of money and how they needed to spend it carefully. Honestly, these words didn't mean anything to me until I was a teenager and began to realize my life would be incomplete without the new Walkman model and a hundred other things. (In case you didn't know, Walkmans were the iPods of our generation.) One of those days when I was throwing a particularly elaborate tantrum, my dad told me something I will never forget. My recollection of that day is strong, partly because of the tone my dad used but also because what he said impacted him. "Money doesn't come for free, nor does it grow on trees. Mom and I need to spend a lot of time to be able to afford everything we do. Remember this, and understand that time is money. Instead of goofing around and complaining, maybe use your time wisely to do something worthwhile."

There are no prizes for guessing what my initial reaction to this speech was! I was obviously mad, but I somewhat understood what Dad was talking about once I calmed down. Both my parents were working, so it was true that they spent most of their days earning money to afford everything we needed at home. Although I hadn't thought about it till then, the value of money is a much more complex concept. You cannot simply evaluate it by the things it can buy.

Coming to the second part of what Dad said, time is money. There are, once again, two ways to interpret things, and it took me a while to figure that out, too. You need to spend time to earn money, so, in a way, time is money. But also, time is a valuable resource, and the more time you have, the better your chances of earning more money. As I grew older, I began to understand what this was all about. In the last chapter, we touched upon the importance of building a habit of saving money right from our teens, but here we will explore the "why" behind that. The sooner you start, the more time you have to accumulate a considerable amount of money with very little effort. If you save only $20 per month at 8% interest per year, in 15 years, you will have saved over $6,500. (*Compound Interest Calculator*, n.d.) I know $6,500 is not a *huge* amount, but it is something when setting aside only $20 monthly. The secret here is compound interest! It sounds intriguing, doesn't it? Keep reading on because, in this chapter, we will be delving deeper into the value of money and the magic of compounding.

WHAT'S A DOLLAR WORTH?

If I ask you how much $100 is worth to you, the first thing you'll probably do is list several things that you can buy with that money. While there is nothing wrong with evaluating money based on the things it can buy, there is more to the story than that.

Instead of focusing on what the value of money entails, let us first talk about why this concept is important. My grandma often said, "Back in our day, you could buy bread for less than a dollar. Look at how prices have increased!" Her comments were my first encounter with the concept of prices increasing over time, which I eventually realized was called inflation. I soon felt the impact of inflation on my life, too. Everything was becoming so expensive that it was getting harder for me to keep up with it. Candies, movies, clothes, and anything else I liked or needed would get more expensive every year. By the time I went to college, I knew exactly what Grandma was talking about.

The Concept of Purchasing Power

Because of inflation and other economic factors, the purchasing power of money reduces over time. In the 1980s, watching a movie would cost around $3.55 without soda and popcorn, but now it is well over $10 (Waggoner, 2020). This means that today, you can no longer buy the same things for $3.55 that you could 30 years ago. This is the concept of purchasing power, and its reduction is an indication that the real value of the dollar has come down. Between 1913 and 2023, the dollar experienced an average inflation rate of 3.17% per year, and that has resulted in a cumulative price increase of around 3,098.91% (Webster, n.d.).

If these numbers seem too far-fetched to you, let's shorten the time horizon to see how rapidly prices are increasing. According to the data published by CoinNews Media Group LLC (2019), the price of a dozen Grade A eggs rose to $2.86 in 2022, which is almost a 71% increase from $1.67 in 2021. These examples illustrate how the purchasing power of a dollar has decreased over the past few years, meaning that a dollar today buys less than it did ten or even five years ago.

There are many reasons behind this periodic decline in the value of the dollar, and one of the most important is that the government has increased the money supply to a great extent in all these years. When the rate of money supply is greater than that of economic growth, the economy faces an inflationary situation. If this sounds a bit over the top, let us break this concept down into simpler terms. The Federal Reserve has the ultimate authority in the United States to increase or decrease the money supply. Suppose the Fed decides to print more money and circulate it in the economy. During the time it takes to make this decision, the economic growth position is unfavorable. This means that goods and services are not being produced at the rate they should be, and there is usually a slowdown in the economy. Think about the COVID-19 pandemic lockdown. Most of the world was closed down, and the result was a global shortage of products and services. In such a time, if the money supply is increased, then technically, there is too much money chasing too few goods. According to the fundamental law of supply and demand, prices will increase when demand is higher than supply.

THE POWER OF COMPOUND INTEREST

While inflation and the saga of ever-increasing prices might seem like a bad thing, it is actually inevitable. Prices are bound to increase as the economy expands and grows more complex. Luckily, there is a foolproof plan to protect yourself against it if you start your personal finance journey right from when you are a teenager.

How Compound Interest Works

Let's face it: We have all studied compound interest in some high school math class, but all was lost in the sea of formulas and complex sums. Don't worry; we will definitely not get into any mathematical formulas. But by the end of this section, you will understand why compound interest is important to your financial success.

Compound interest, or compounding, is a process where you earn interest on the money that you invested plus previous interest earned on that money. Stay with me while I explain this to you more clearly. When you're investing with the hopes of earning interest on your deposit, there are two aspects to such an investment:

- **The Principal**: The initial deposit(s) you make to start the investment. It also includes any subsequent deposit that you make into your account.
- **The Interest**: This is the income you earn from the money you deposited, usually represented by a percentage. At the end of each year, you keep the money in the investment account and receive interest income, which is added to the principal. As a result, the accumulated balance in your account increases every year.

When your money is compounding, you earn interest on the principal and the accumulated interest that you have already earned. This means that, technically, you are earning interest on interest. If you keep depositing a certain amount of money every year, it will soon start growing phenomenally over time. In fact, if you simply deposit some money once, compounding will still reap enormous benefits for you because the interest will keep on accumulating!

Pros and Cons of Compounding

Let me start this section by saying that there are absolutely no cons to compounding from an investment perspective, except for one particular situation. If you have not kept the money in a tax-sheltered account, then you will need to pay taxes on the return you earn from compounding. But I would not call it a drawback because paying taxes on your income is a very normal and expected thing to do.

The biggest advantage of compounding is that it helps you grow your money significantly faster with regular deposits. You are earning further returns on the returns you have already earned, and your money is increasing rapidly over time. Moreover, the interest rate you earn as a part of long-term compounding is usually greater than the existing inflation rate in the economy. As a result, your money remains intact, and your wealth becomes future-proof. Economic factors like the high cost of living and the declining purchasing power of money have a lesser chance of eroding it away.

From a non-investment point of view, compounding can become a problem on loans that charge compound interest. Consider the tables turned, and instead of investments, you owe a certain sum of money, and you'll have to pay interest on the debt. You are supposed to repay a certain amount every month. Still, your creditor is charging interest on the amount that is due. Over time, they would charge interest on interest, making your debt more than it initially was. This is a common occurrence, especially in the case of credit cards.

Why Starting Early Is the Best Solution

I am sure by now you are already convinced about the magic of compounding and the massive benefits it can bring you. You'll notice that I kept using the words "over time" while discussing the phenomenal returns that can be earned from compound interest. This is because compound interest becomes all the more beneficial over a longer time horizon. I know I said you won't need to do any math, but here's a straightforward numerical example so I can demonstrate what compound interest looks like over time.

Suppose you opened an investment account by depositing $1,000, and you plan on depositing the same amount every year. The account pays compound interest at 8% per year. Let's quickly look at how your returns will grow over the next five years.

	Year 1	Year 2	Year 3	Year 4	Year 5
Opening Balance ($)	0	1080	2246	3506	4866
Deposit ($)	1,000	1000	1000	1000	1000
Total Amount on Which Interest Will Be Received (Opening Balance + Deposit)	1000	2080	3246	4506	5866
(+) Interest at 8% ($)	80	166	260	360	469
Closing Balance ($)	1080	2246	3506	4866	6335

To get a better visual of the above investment, let's look at the line graph below.

Investment Growth with $1000 Annual Contributions Over 5 Years at 8% Annual Interest

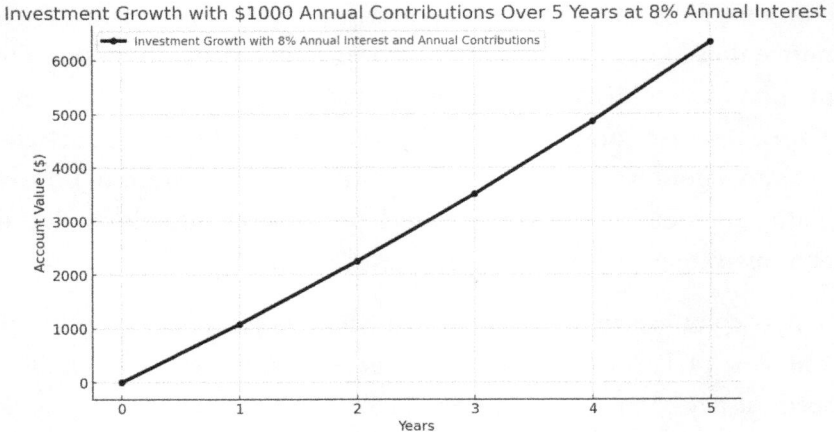

You can see how rapidly the interest amounts have increased over the course of these five years. If you maintain a steady investment amount every year, your returns will keep rising as time passes. Consider how much money you can save by depositing $1,000 per year (which is less than $100 per month) if you start in your teenage years. The reason why investing early is the most effective way to utilize compound interest is because time is in your favor, and you can create a huge fund with relatively little effort. Setting aside $100 from your allowance might seem like too much at the moment, but that amount will soon be highly achievable for you once you get a job. For now, you can always ask your parents to help you and give you a head start. Trust me, you'll be thanking yourself later on.

REAL-LIFE MONEY STORIES

There are numerous instances of teens and young adults benefiting from the magic of compound interest. Let's look at the story of Aaron Shapiro, Founder and CEO of Carver Edison in New York City. Aaron mentioned that, as a child, he used to set aside a few cents in a jar every day so he could buy the things he wanted. This is one of the most common ways to start a savings habit, and it worked really well for Aaron. Over time, the few cents in the jar turned to a few dollars every day because the things that Aaron wanted were becoming more and more expensive. Thankfully, he did not stop this activity as he grew older. In fact, the habit grew with him and evolved into automatic savings, recurring deposits, and investment accounts. Aaron firmly believes that these good money habits can easily be built from a young age, and starting early is beneficial, too.

Aaron's story proves that when you start saving and investing at a young age, the habit becomes much easier to build. Money management becomes an organic activity in your life instead of something you are scared of doing. As you grow older, you look forward to financial management and increasing your expertise, even if you do not get a degree in business or finance.

THE DOS AND DON'TS OF MANAGING COMPOUND INTEREST ACCOUNTS

Compound interest has multiple benefits, and the earlier you start, the better your chances of using it optimally. But I also want to touch upon one of the less talked-about issues related to compound interest. You can open an investment account in the hopes of earning high returns in the long run but still not be able to get the desired results if you are not managing your account correctly.

So, in this section, I will list some essential dos and don'ts to ensure you are getting the most out of compound interest.

Dos	Don'ts
• **Open an investment account that pays compound interest in your teens.**	• Procrastinate and delay your savings plan. The longer you wait, the harder it will be to start, so be proactive and open the account today.
• **Keep depositing a fixed amount of money every month. This can be a certain percentage of your monthly income or allowance.**	• Take any money out of that investment account prematurely. The whole point of compound interest is to allow your money to grow by earning interest by accumulating principal and interest. The benefits of compounding would be defeated if you took money out of that account.
• **Reinvest the interest back into the investment account to enjoy the phenomenal returns of compounding.**	• Withdraw the interest or use your investment account as a checking account. These two should be separate, and the only transaction that you should make in the investment account is the periodic deposit.
• **Make it a habit to consistently add to your investment account to grow your funds steadily and increase the amount periodically. For example, you can start saving $100 per month and then, the next year, increase it to $110 per month or even more if it is affordable.**	• Make the savings process irregular. Sporadic or infrequent savings can disrupt the compounding process, leading to less growth.

• **Use online tools like compound interest calculators to project your savings growth over time. (For your information, the one on the U.S. Securities and Exchange Commission website is one of the most accurate and easy-to-use compound interest calculators, so make sure to check that out!)**	• Guess your growth and end up overestimating or underestimating. The whole point of financial literacy is to be aware of how your money is growing and working for you.
• **Be patient and realize that growing wealth through compound interest takes time.**	• Have unrealistic expectations about compounding. Your money is not going to double itself in a month, and if you are hoping that is going to happen, it will only lead to disappointment.

Understanding the value of money can be a complex concept. The dollar's value has changed and been reduced multiple times over the years and will continue to do so in the future. The value of money is a dynamic concept. Still, one constant thing is the importance of time in future-proofing your finances. The sooner you start saving, the greater the impact of compounding will be. But to reap the maximum benefits of compound interest, you must take active steps to build a sizable savings fund. In the next chapter, we will discuss some specialized savings strategies designed for teens that will help you maximize your savings, make your money work, and grow for you.

3

SMART SAVING STRATEGIES

"Money, like emotions, is something you must
control to keep your life on the right track."

— NATASHA MUNSON

As someone who grew up in a very modest financial situation, I've had a bittersweet relationship with savings for the longest time. Like most children, I grew up hearing about "savings" and the "need to save" in bits and pieces of conversation between my parents. When I was young, they never taught me how to save money or why it is essential, but they did emphasize that it should be done. I don't blame them because financial literacy among teens wasn't really a thing back then. In fact, my parents were also not taught how to manage their money, and it was something they learned while dealing with their finances.

As I grew older, I was always in two minds about saving money, especially after I started working part-time after school. I could hear my parents' ominous reminders about how savings could be life-changing. Still, on the other hand, there was also the pressure of appearing cool in front of my friends. If everyone was buying something, I had to do that too, and savings would take a backseat. I knew saving was essential and something I needed to do, but the problem was I wasn't sure about the "why." Since I couldn't figure out the rationale, I would often skip saving money and instead spend it on something I wanted but didn't need. I continued this sporadic savings spree until I had a medical emergency in my senior year of college. I sprained my right elbow badly while playing basketball. While it wasn't severe, it prevented me from working my part-time job of waiting tables at the on-campus diner for over six weeks. I was lucky enough that I wasn't fired while I was recovering. Still, those few weeks were extremely hard for me, both physically and financially. I didn't want to ask my parents for help, and for the first couple of weeks, I tried to manage on my own until I realized that I hadn't saved any money for such an emergency. Eventually, I caved and called my mom for help. She visited bearing cookies, lasagna, and some much-needed wisdom about saving money for emergencies like this one. I didn't argue because I knew she was right, and I was in the wrong. I could have easily saved a few weeks' worth of living expenses if I maintained a steady savings rate and didn't spend money on random things.

When you're young and you don't have much money, under-standing the reasoning behind saving money can seem confusing because you really cannot see how the future will look. Moreover, it can be difficult to maintain composure when you face intense peer pressure. But you've got to prioritize savings over something you do with the money after buying everything you want. I will share some proven saving strategies designed specifically for teenagers in this chapter. You will gain the knowledge to manage your allowances or part-time job incomes, the importance of an emergency fund, and how to navigate the tricky waters of peer pressure so you can make more informed financial decisions.

THE 50-30-20 RULE FOR TEENS

I'll be honest: Starting a savings journey is definitely not easy, especially if you are still on an allowance or have just begun a part-time job. The common notion is that saving is not possible when you don't have too much money, and this belief prevents most teenagers from saving. This is not true because, even though you are not making or receiving large amounts of money, you also have significantly fewer responsibilities. Think about it: If you still live with your parents, they cover most of the household expenses. Even if you have moved out to pursue a college degree, you don't have as many expenses to bear while living alone. So even if you are not making a lot of money, you don't have the responsibilities of a 40-year-old married person with two kids, and you should definitely make the most of it by starting your savings journey.

The easiest way to start a savings habit is to follow the 50-30-20 rule. This is a popular budgeting strategy where you dedicate 50% of your total income toward your needs or essential bills, 30% toward wants, and the remaining 20% is saved. Setting aside money for your needs and wants makes saving much more accessible. In case this sounds a bit confusing, follow this step-by-step guide to use the 50-30-20 rule efficiently:

1. Track how much money you are making. If you're still on an allowance, your total income would only consist of the amount you receive from your parents. If you have a job, make sure to include your income and any other amount you get regularly.

2. Find out how much money you are spending every month. Using a budgeting app to track your spending is a good idea because most expenses are online. Apps make it easier for us to keep tabs on our regular expenses, and you can easily categorize them to get insight into where your money is going.

3. Based on the categories created by your budgeting app, you can figure out your needs and wants. In case you need to be aware, needs are those expenses that are absolutely essential for your survival, like rent, utilities, gas, etc. On the other hand, wants are avoidable expenses, but they improve the quality of your life. Examples of wants include the latest iPhone, an expensive pair of shoes, or something else you have wanted to own for a while.

4. Once you determine how much money you are spending on each category, you will be better positioned to determine how much you can save comfortably. Ideally, your needs should be around 50% of your income, and your wants should not exceed 30%.

5. Create a budgeting plan according to your determined expenses so you can easily save 20% of your monthly income. To make this process really work for you, ensure you are sticking to it.

6. Review this plan every few months to ensure you are on track. Financial management plans must be dynamic, so you should quickly make changes according to your needs.

Benefits of the 50-30-20 Rule

The 50-30-20 rule is one of the most efficient ways to start a budgeting and savings journey. Of course, this is not the only strategy, and you can explore other options too! But here are a few reasons that make it very suitable, especially for teenagers:

- First and foremost, it is an easy-to-use and straightforward strategy. You don't have to think too hard about what is happening and quickly get into the habit of financial management. Simplicity is underrated but highly efficient, and the 50-30-20 rule is an excellent example of this philosophy.
- Even if you are not meeting any significant expenses now, this rule gives you insight into your needs and wants. Dedicating 50% of your income toward needs helps you identify and prioritize the essential expenses of your life. This budgeting strategy also points out that the money spent on your wants should always be less than what you spend on essentials.
- By specifying a 20% rate for savings, this strategy helps you quickly get into the habit of saving money. You can set this amount aside the moment you receive your pay or allowance because you already know how much you will be spending on your essentials and your wants.
- Finally, this rule helps you establish a financial balance by promoting a healthy mix of expenses and savings. Since you are allocating money for the things you want, this budgeting strategy won't feel restrictive.

How You Can Customize the Rule According to Your Needs

Most teens don't have to contribute to household necessities. If you are among that group, you are at a significant advantage in increasing your savings rate beyond the prescribed 20%. As a teenager, you wouldn't usually have high bills and should be able to save more, based on percentage, than an adult.

In this context, it is important to understand that needs and wants can often be subjective, depending on your personal choices and situations. Just like you should aim to save at a higher rate if you can, you shouldn't feel defeated if your present situation does not allow you to save 20%. Start with a rate you can comfortably achieve and maintain for some time, then gradually increase when you feel comfortable doing so. The idea here is to learn to build a savings habit. While it is important to save as much as you can, it is also essential that you don't get overwhelmed.

Before you start following the 50-30-20 rule, take a moment to understand what your needs and wants look like. Let me give you an example of how these things can be subjective. If you play a sport like baseball or basketball, staying fit is an integral part of your life. A pair of good sports shoes and a gym membership might be a necessity for you. On the other hand, if you are not into sports and mostly enjoy being indoors, these expenses might not even be present in the "wants" category.

If you're still at home and don't have to pay for many of the "needs," try to save at least 50% of your income or allowance. That way, your savings journey will get a head start for your future. If you maintain a high savings rate until you move out and have to pay for more things, you will have saved quite a lot of money even before you start an actual job. Combined with the power of compounding, you'll see your money growing in no time!

Importance of Savings

As adults, we often take pride in doing things correctly, compared to children and young adults. That's how it's supposed to be, right? Adults are supposed to know better and act better, but more often than not, that is not the case. Let me share an interesting statistic in the context of savings. As of August 2023, the personal savings rate for American individuals was 3.9% (Whiteside, 2023). This is much less than the prescribed 20%. Not everyone can afford to save 20% of their income, which is absolutely understandable. But apart from the affordability factor, another primary reason behind this number is that most American adults do not have a habit of saving money.

Even if you get a business degree and a very high-paying job, you need to be more efficient in maintaining a steady savings rate. This is where the 50-30-20 rule comes in handy. You don't have to overthink it; simply start setting aside 20% of your income, and you'll be set. If you discover that 20% is a tall target for you, then evaluate the money you are spending toward your needs and wants and fix another rate accordingly.

BUILDING YOUR FIRST EMERGENCY FUND

When you're young, it is almost impossible to imagine emergencies. You stay with your parents, and there's usually a protective cocoon surrounding you. That is why imagining how you'd react in such a situation is challenging. Taking any active steps to prepare for it is even more challenging. This is precisely what happened to me when I hurt myself in college. Being a sportsperson, I had gotten injured plenty of times before. Still, I only felt the whole impact of it then.

The deal with emergencies is that you can never be truly mentally prepared to deal with them, which makes them so scary. But you can prepare yourself financially, and let me tell you this; it will save you a lot of trouble. We don't have control over how we feel when something unexpected happens. Still, we do have the power to ensure that we are able to handle financial issues. Trust me, things will look much worse if you are struggling financially during a crisis. So, as a responsible person, start a plan to build an emergency fund so you don't have to worry too much on the financial side.

Before delving deeper into the topic, let us first understand what an emergency fund is. An emergency fund, often called a rainy-day fund, is money you set aside for any emergency. This can include sudden job loss, medical issues that are preventing you from working, or anything that might cause a more-than-usual strain on your finances. It is essential to understand when to use this fund, and you should be careful not to misuse it. You will be tempted to spend it on things you want, like that new dress or a phone. But remember the reason behind creating this fund before you spend the money on random things.

The purpose of having such a fund is that you will be financially protected in an emergency and will not need to dip into your savings or, worse, opt for loans to pay for your expenses.

Steps to Build

The concept of an emergency fund sounds perfect in theory. However, the implementation can be tricky, especially if you're still on your allowance or have just started a part-time job. The process can be slightly different for you based on your situation. Still, there are some common steps you can follow for building an emergency fund for the first time:

- **Fix an Amount**: Finance experts suggest that you should have at least three to six months of living expenses as your emergency fund. Calculating your monthly living expenses is easy if you have already moved out of your parent's home. Add up everything under the "needs" category and multiply that by three (or six) to get the amount you have to save. If you're still at home, it might be a good idea to talk to your parents before deciding on an amount for your emergency fund. You can think about saving half of your allowance or what you make from your part-time job (if you have one). You can also opt for a specific amount, like $1,000 or $1,500, and aim toward achieving that goal over a certain period.

- **Start Small**: The challenging part of creating an emergency fund is figuring out how to start saving for it. We already talked about maintaining a 20% savings rate. Hence, should the money for your emergency fund come out of that 20%, or do you need to set more money aside for it? The answer will depend on your current level of responsibility. If 20% is the maximum that you can save, then you will have to set aside a part of that until the fund is created. On the other hand, if you can save more, use the additional savings to build your fund first. Starting with a small amount is a good idea, so it doesn't seem overwhelming.
- **Create a Separate Account**: The money where you keep your emergency savings should be separate from your regular checking account. The point is to ensure you are not spending this money even accidentally. In the next section, we will discuss the types of accounts for your emergency savings.
- **Contribute Regularly**: Like all savings plans, make sure to contribute regularly to your emergency fund. Even if it is a small amount, like $20, remember to make a consistent monthly deposit so you can prioritize it.

Setting up a Separate Savings Account for Your Emergency Fund

Making a plan to create an emergency fund is the first step, but you also need to ensure that you keep the fund safe and not use it for non-emergencies. That is why the Consumer Financial Protection Bureau (CFPB) suggests setting up a different savings account for your emergency fund (CapitalOne, 2023). The idea is to make sure the funds are accessible but not so accessible that you dip into them whenever you feel like it. If you are looking to create a separate account for your emergency savings, here are a few options:

- **Traditional Savings Account**: Opening a second savings account is an excellent idea for setting aside your emergency money. You can also open a certificate of deposit (CD), which is a time-bound deposit account. The money will stay blocked in this account for a specified period, after which you can withdraw it. CDs also pay a higher rate of interest in comparison to traditional savings accounts, which makes them a suitable option for building emergency funds.
- **Money Market Account**: This is similar to a high-yield savings account. Even though the interest rates are higher, you might not be able to withdraw the money easily compared to traditional savings accounts. But that works out perfectly when you're using it to save for emergencies. The only problem with these accounts is that you need a minimum amount to open and maintain them. If you don't have the money at first, you can ask your parents to help make the initial deposit. You can always pay them back later.
- **Low-Risk Investment Account**: This is a less traditional suggestion, but using a low-risk investment account is a great place to store your emergency savings. Investing in financial instruments like bonds can help you simultaneously earn an income while you are setting up your emergency fund. However, it is important to choose a low-risk option so your money can stay intact. If you invest your emergency fund in stocks, it will make your money vulnerable to stock market fluctuations.

Once you have finalized an option, you'll have to ensure that you are funding the account regularly. The best way to do that is by setting up automatic transfers through a budgeting app or your bank's internal recurring transfer system. Automating your savings will help you stay on track with your financial goals and ensure you remember to save. Even if you have the best intentions, saving money can sometimes take a backseat. Life happens, and when a lot is going on, you might simply forget to save, even if you want to. Automatic savings will take that pressure off. You can build your savings funds without worrying about having to transfer money manually every month.

PEER PRESSURE VS. YOUR WALLET: MAKING SMART CHOICES

It's not always easy to keep calm when you see your friends having fun and enjoying things you don't have. Peer pressure can take a significant toll on our mental health and finances if we are not carefully addressing the issue. I know this because I have been on its sticky end and have made some questionable financial decisions under the influence of my friends. I was a freshman in college when some of my friends planned a hiking trip during a long weekend. It was one of those trips where everyone was going, and since it was just the beginning of our college days, missing might mean I'd get excluded from all the groups later on. So I agreed to go. But frankly, I did not have the money for the trip. So, I used some of the funds my parents gave me to get me through the first few days of college until I got a part-time job. Luckily, I got a job during my first week, so I didn't need to use my parents' money. It wasn't a lot, but it was enough to get me by for at least a few weeks. I used up all the money on the trip and even bought some hiking gear so my classmates could see how cool I was.

The trip was amazing, but the consequences of the money I spent were far less impressive. After I got back, I realized I wouldn't get paid for another week, and I barely had any money to meet even my basic needs. I couldn't ask my parents, so I took an extra shift at work. I barely had any time for studying, and my grades took a hit—all for a hiking trip. The hardships that I had to face made me understand that it really wasn't worth it. I'm not saying I never made any bad decisions ever since, but this incident gave me a reality check.

The teens of today have it even more challenging than before. Social media has made the impact of peer pressure worse because you are constantly connected to other people and looking at what they are doing. Moreover, most people pretend to be happier on social media than they actually are, which makes the FOMO even more real. Young adults have a hard time dealing with all these emotions. There is a constant urge to fit in with their peers by making the same lifestyle choices, even if those choices are heavy on the pocket. If these feelings seem relatable to you, don't beat yourself up. It is normal to feel this way, but it is important to identify them and take actionable steps to escape the trap of peer pressure.

Striking a balance between spending to fit in and sticking to your budget is essential if you want to achieve long-term financial independence. To do that, you must first build a positive and healthy relationship with money. Whenever you feel that you need money to fit in with a particular group of people, remember this mantra: Money or the lack of it should not determine your relationship with anybody. If it does, then you probably need to re-evaluate those relationships because these are not the kind of people you want to surround yourself with. I know it sounds a bit harsh, but it is one of the harder pills to swallow when you're trying to become financially independent.

Stick to your needs and wants, and always remember that if an expense is wrecking your budget, then you should not be making it. The temptations can be hard to resist, but you need to remind yourself of your priorities and values. You can always spend a little extra if it aligns with your life goals and if it's genuinely important to you. Let me give you an example of a teenager called Sofi Cruz Turner, who saved money to buy things for her friend Jahiem when she saw he was in dire need. Sofi is a high school student from North Carolina, and she saved money from her job and a little contribution from her parents. Jahiem had been Sofi's friend since third grade, and when he asked if anyone could help with buying a new pair of shoes, Sofi stepped up and bought him shoes, clothes, and a new backpack. This instance proves that using your saved-up money for a genuine cause is always okay.

INTERACTIVE ELEMENT: SAVINGS CALENDAR

Taking that first step toward saving money is one of the most challenging and important lessons on your path to financial independence and freedom. That is why I am going to give you a slight nudge to help you get started. Here is a fun activity in the form of a savings calendar. The challenge is to start with $1 on day one and increase by a dollar daily. You can save the money in a jar or a bank account, where you'd deposit the money every day. If you can follow the plan rigorously, at the end of 30 days, you will have saved $465. That is quite an achievement, and you get bonus points for making an effort to build a savings habit.

In the table below, write down how much you are saving in each box and make a total at the end of every week to keep yourself motivated on this journey. This is what it should look like:

Day 0: $1, Day 1: $2, Day 2: $3, Day 3: $4, and so on.

Day 0	1	2	3	4	5	6	Total Savings This Week
8	9	10	11	12	13	14	
15	16	17	18	19	20	21	
22	23	24	25	26	27	28	
29	30						

Learning to save money is one of the first and most important lessons on your path toward becoming financially independent. But let me drop a truth bomb here: Saving every penny every chance you get is not always feasible. While you can make it a point to build a systematic savings habit, you must also ensure your spending choices align with that habit. It's not enough to keep saving; you'll also have to ensure that you are making the right decisions when it comes to spending money. That is why, in the next chapter, we will explore the ins and outs of spending wisely so you never have to feel remorse after paying for something you bought!

SMART SPENDING FOR SAVVY TEENS

"I was raised to have value for money, to have respect for money, even though you have a lot of it."

— JENNIFER LAWRENCE

Jacob, my roommate in college, was an extraordinary cook. This was a remarkable feat, given that we had access to very limited cooking accessories. Jacob would whip up delicious meals even with minimal ingredients and keep us all well-fed. (After finishing his finance degree, he pursued his passion and became a chef, so you can imagine his talent!)

Even though Jacob was the dorm hero for his meals, he was also famous for something else. He had a severe addiction to buying things in bulk or things that were not even remotely necessary for any college student. For instance, he would stock up on gourmet cheeses, ten different kinds of sauces, fresh herbs, and pastry crusts. He even bought a cast iron pan once because it was supposedly on sale. For your information, we did not even have a proper kitchen, and he could not use that pan. Jacob justified his purchases by saying that his passion for cooking made him do it. Although his passion was definitely strong, he would often face financial problems because of his impulse buys. He had to borrow money from us often, too, and we would help him as much as we could because of all the great food he was cooking. But that wasn't a sustainable solution, and Jacob was almost always in debt and struggled to make ends meet.

As you grow older and start making more money, you'll have plenty of opportunities to buy things that you want. There is nothing wrong with indulging yourself, but here's the thing you need to remember: Just because you can afford to buy it doesn't mean you have to. Setting spending boundaries and making financial decisions rationally are super skills that will come in very handy in the future. There is no point in resisting yourself because, at some point, your temptations will get the better of you. Instead, try to understand the difference between what you truly need and what is just a fleeting want. In this chapter, we will discuss strategies to master the art of smart spending so you can become more self-aware about your spending habits, laying the foundation for wise financial decisions in the future.

THE WANTS VS. NEEDS DILEMMA

We briefly discussed the concept of wants and needs while talking about the 50-30-20 budgeting strategy in the previous chapter. Needs and wants can be subjective and often vary greatly depending on the type of person you are and the lifestyle choices you make. Nevertheless, the following ground rules can help you understand the difference between needs and wants.

- Needs are those that you "need" for survival. Think about it this way: If you're trapped on an island what are the basic things that you would need to stay alive and healthy? Food, clothing, and shelter. Needs usually revolve around these three things and include certain additional things like medicines, insurance, and transportation costs.
- Wants are all about the extra stuff you wish to have. They're not essential for your survival, but they're nice to have and can make life more enjoyable. Some examples include the latest phone, game console, vacations, eating out, and hobbies you are into.

In this context, it is worth mentioning that many people want to play a huge role in their mental well-being. In such cases, the lines between needs and wants can be quite blurry, and it might be confusing to differentiate between them.

Making a Self-Aware Purchase Decision

What you need vs. what you want should play a significant role in every purchase decision you make. The ultimate objective is to ensure you are not spending money on things you don't need (or even want). To achieve that, here are a few things that you should keep on your mental checklist:

1. Evaluate whether the thing you want to purchase is a "need" or a "want". You already know what these two mean, so you should be able to differentiate between them. In case you are still confused, ask yourself if this item is essential for your survival or well-being. If the answer is yes, then there is a need. You don't need to second-guess your choices, especially when it comes to things that really

matter to you. Trust yourself to categorize the needs correctly.

2. If the thing you want to buy is a want, then ask yourself some questions before buying it. For example, how will you use the item? Is this something that you will be using on a daily basis? Why do you want to purchase it, or what are you missing out on if you don't own it? Do you think this item will be useful or relevant after a year? The answers to these questions will help you understand if your purchase is justified or if you're doing it out of impulse.

3. You must determine whether a purchase will be cost-effective if the answers to the abovementioned questions show that impulse is not driving your decision. Here, you have to determine whether you can actually afford the item. Suppose this is an essential item, and you have dedicated 40% of your income or allowance toward your needs. How much of that 40% will you be spending if you decide to go ahead with the purchase? I know it sounds like a lot, but if you are spending a large portion of the money allocated toward wants on a single thing, then it is an indication that the item might be too expensive for you.

4. Before making the final decision, sleep on it or give it at least 24 hours. Think about it: It's the middle of the night, and you are scrolling through Instagram when you come across an Amazon link to a set of scented candles. The deal is excellent, and you really like the aesthetic of scented candles in your room. It's not a need, but it is something you want to buy. However, you can see that despite the discounts, the price is high, and you might end up spending most of the money you have allocated for wants if you go through with the purchase. You can see that this price is a "limited period offer," which will expire

after half an hour. In such a case, the best course of action is to wait until morning and see if you still feel the same urge to buy it. More often than not, you'll realize that you didn't actually want it, but it was just a heat-of-the-moment temptation. By allowing yourself some time before going through with the purchase, you will be in a better position to justify and make sense of your decisions.

In this context, I want to emphasize the importance of being confident in your decisions. Just because you are not an adult yet doesn't automatically mean all the purchase decisions you are making are wrong. Needs and wants vary over time, and something that might not be on your priority list at the moment might end up becoming an essential expense in a few years. You know what your needs are, so remember to be true to yourself, and your decisions will automatically start making more sense.

SETTING SPENDING BOUNDARIES

Setting boundaries is not something that we usually associate with positive things. Right from our childhood, we've been taught to gain limitless knowledge or put in endless hours of work to achieve something. The only time we are asked to set "limits" is when we are supposedly doing something wrong. For example, "Don't watch too much TV," "Don't eat too much junk food," or "Don't stare at your phone for so long." Quite naturally, we tend to relate the concept of setting boundaries to something negative or restrictive. As a result, whenever we talk about cutting back or setting spending limits, our minds immediately associate it with feelings like "This means I won't be able to have any fun anymore." Let me bust this myth for you right here, right now. Spending within specified limits does not mean you have to stop having fun.

In fact, it can make it easier for you to have fun and buy all the things you want. Let's discover how.

Budgeting and Accountability

The first step toward setting healthy spending boundaries is creating a budget. A budget is a plan that lists your income, expenses, and estimates for each expense category. This means you're not just listing out how much you are spending; you are also noting how much you *should be spending.* This process helps you understand the gaps between actual and estimated expenses. It allows you to evaluate the reasons behind the gap.

Creating a budget also helps you track your expenses more efficiently and set more realistic estimates for yourself. Most of the time, we are under the impression that we don't spend as much as we actually do. This is one of the primary reasons why we end up overspending and losing track of our expenses. Suppose you buy lunch from the high school cafeteria every day, which costs around $3. This means you spend over $60 on lunch every month. However, while preparing your first budget, you allocate $75 toward your monthly expenses on food without considering that most of the money is being spent on your school lunch. This will leave you with only $15 for all your other food-related expenses for the month, which might not be enough.

If you're not aware of how much you are spending on each category, there is no way for you to know if you are going over the limit. In fact, you won't even be able to set proper limits for each of your expenses. Budgeting helps you understand your expenses and be accountable for the money you are spending. Remember this: Accountability is not limited to your allowance. You might be answerable to your parents today, but pretty soon, you'll be on your own and spending your hard-earned money. If you start budgeting at a young age, it will become easier for you to stay true to your values and spend wisely.

Don't Be Afraid to Have Difficult Conversations

A big part of setting spending limits is having a healthy relationship with money. Whenever you feel like your budget is being too restrictive, remember the following things:

- The budget is not set in stone. You can always make changes to it as your needs change. This does not mean you will modify your budget whenever you want to buy something. Still, it implies that you can modify some estimates if your situation has changed significantly.
- You are not doing anyone any favors by sticking to your budget. As I said before, it's your money, and if you manage it efficiently, you'll be in a better financial position.

Most teenagers do not consider budgeting to be an important activity because they are not used to the concept. Parents usually do not like to involve their kids in conversations about money. Subsequently, kids tend to feel that it is taboo to talk about finances. If you can relate to this feeling, then you need to do the hard thing and ask your parents to break this cycle. Instead of telling them they are wrong not to include you in these discussions, let them know how beneficial it would be for you if you knew about the basics of money management.

I know bringing things up with parents can seem intimidating, but trust me, they want to help you as much as they can. An open line of communication will help you become more confident about managing money from a young age. It is very important to remove the awkwardness and get comfortable with things like budgeting, saving, investing, and dealing with your own income. Once you know what you are working for, you won't feel like your budget is holding you back, and setting spending boundaries will come more naturally.

HOW TO NAVIGATE AND RESIST TEMPTATION

Let's face it: We are all a little addicted to online window shopping. Who wouldn't be? There are so many websites and apps and so many options to choose from. You can spend hours looking at all the amazing things that are available, be it clothes, gadgets, skincare, food, or literally anything else. No matter how many spending boundaries you set or how strict you are about your finances, resisting temptation can be pretty hard.

I'll be honest with you: Making a budget is one of the most helpful ways to resist the urge to buy impulsively. When you stick to a budget for a while, you eventually get mentally invested in saving a portion of your income. With time, you'll even get the urge to dabble in different types of investment options and get more serious about managing your money. But this entire process takes time to happen, and unless you can nip the habit of impulse shopping in the bud, you might not even be able to get to the budgeting stage. So here are a few quick tips that will help you keep your impulse spending urges under control:

- Shift your perspective about the cost of the item you wish to buy. Usually, we try to look at it from the point of view of how much money we are spending on it. Instead, try to think about how long it will take you to earn that money. Suppose you have a job that pays you $10 per hour, and you want to buy a pair of fancy shoes that cost $100. Do you think those shoes are worth 10 hours of your time?

The moment you start measuring the value of items according to time, you'll realize the actual impact impulse spending is having on your finances.

- Make it more challenging for yourself to actually go through with a purchase. Don't save your payment information so that you'll have to manually add the information every time you have to buy something. It doesn't sound like much, but you cannot imagine how lazy we can get if we have to fill in all those details every time. There is a good chance that you'll abandon the purchase.

- Gamify the experience of not buying. You can do a no-spend challenge or a buying cleanse where you won't buy anything for a specific period, like a few weeks or a month. At the end of the challenge, you can reward yourself by buying something you like.

- Don't compare yourself with your peers or anyone else. One of the major reasons we buy things impulsively is because we see someone we know owning the same thing. I understand it can feel pretty rough when you see others living a luxurious life. Still, you need to remember that your journey is different from theirs. You have your own set of goals and financial objectives that your friend might not relate to. It is hard to eliminate comparison completely, but it's a process worth starting in your teens.

- Cut yourself some slack and indulge in impulse buying once in a while. If you keep following a fad diet for a long period of time, there is a high chance that your cravings will get the better of you. Sooner or later, you'll be so frustrated with the salads and smoothies that you'll end up breaking the entire discipline and getting into the rabbit hole of binge eating. Similarly, if you keep denying yourself the joys of an impulse buy, the cravings will kick in soon and make you buy things you'll regret. Impulse buying is called a guilty pleasure for a reason, so be kind to yourself and have some fun.

Delayed Gratification for the Win

While we're talking about impulse shopping, it is worth discussing the concept of instant gratification that comes with it. When you buy something impulsively, there's this moment of instant happiness that follows the purchase. It's similar to the feeling you get after eating a bag of candy or cheesecake. Instant gratification is a very powerful emotion, and it is what makes us do things impulsively. The sensation is divine, but it doesn't last long before guilt, regret, and other negative emotions take their place. That is why, if you're considering addressing your impulse shopping habit, you'll need to evaluate your feelings surrounding instant gratification.

I know it can be challenging, but you have to look at the bigger picture. More often than not, pursuing instant gratification results in bad decisions, and I'm not just talking about money. Let me give you an example. Suppose you're working part-time at the local cafe, where your main job is to wait tables and stay at the counter for an hour. One day, your colleague took a day off, and things got really busy at the counter, which caused some delays in taking orders. Your manager put the entire blame on you and behaved very rudely in front of customers, even though you were trying your level best to get things done correctly. In such a situation, you have every right to feel infuriated and even be tempted to quit the job. Quitting would make you feel good because the manager's behavior was unjustified. This is where the dangers of instant gratification come into the picture. The job is probably helping you financially, and even though quitting might make you feel good for the moment, it might have a negative impact in the long run.

No matter what situation you are facing in life, before making a decision, always take a moment to evaluate the consequences. Of course, there can always be exceptions, but this rule applies to most things. Try to practice delayed gratification or the act of holding out today for a better reward in the future. This will work for you in all spheres of life, not just financial management. If you avoid buying something impulsively today, you can use the money you saved for something far better in the future. You can even start a journal where you make a note every time you stop yourself from making an impulse purchase about how much money you saved. After you have added more than ten items to the list, add up how much you have saved and what big purchases you can make with that money.

INTERACTIVE ELEMENT

Keeping track of your spending can help you build accountability and identify any problematic patterns that might be stopping you from achieving your true financial potential. That is why it is a good idea to maintain a spending diary where you'll note down your purchases and mention why you spent the money on that item. Remember, the point is not to shame yourself for buying things but to understand areas for improvement. The blame game will simply fill you with negativity and won't let you properly get the job done.

Here is a simple spending diary that you can fill out for a week and evaluate your decisions. To spice it up a bit, choose a week when you know you might spend more than usual, like during the holidays or the week before your birthday. This will help you further identify any typical trends your spending decisions exhibit.

Day	Item You Bought	Price in Dollars	Need or Want	Why You Bought It
1				
2				
3				
4				
5				
6				
7				

Reflect on anything in particular that you observed as you documented all your expenses this week. Why did you make some of the spending decisions that you did? Could they be avoided? Look for areas of improvement and make a note of them in the box below.

Spending wisely is one of the most essential financial management skills you must master. In your teens, it is easy to "stop spending money at all" to exercise financial control. But that is not a sustainable habit, especially in the long run. Sure, you could not spend any money for a month or two, but is that feasible after that? No. You will have bills to pay and things to buy. Money management becomes much simpler once you understand how to spend wisely because all of your decisions are based on reason rather than emotion. In fact, once you get a grip on spending wisely, you'll feel more confident to start eyeing some big-ticket items like that laptop for school or even your dream car. In the next chapter, we will learn how to plan and save for those significant purchases without breaking the bank.

MAPPING OUT BIG PURCHASES

"To make an embarrassing admission, I like video games. That's what got me into software engineering when I was a kid. I wanted to make money so I could buy a better computer to play better video games - nothing like saving the world."

— ELON MUSK

As you grow older, you'll experience a ton of new things. Getting into college, completing a degree, getting your first "adult" job, meeting the love of your life, getting married, getting your first pet, having your first child, and many other things that will enrich your life. As these events keep happening, you will get a taste of adulthood. For most people, this comes across more like a shock than a surprise because they are not prepared for what life is about to throw at them. After all, who can predict how they will feel when they realize they have met their soulmate? Or how can someone even guess what it feels like to work over forty hours a week until they start a corporate job?

It's not just the emotions that come as a surprise; most adults are thoroughly confused and lost when it comes to making financial decisions, too. When we are living with our parents, we don't think about the big expenses because, at the back of our minds, we know Mom and Dad will take care of them. There is absolutely nothing wrong with depending on your parents. Still, you should also be aware of how big financial decisions are made. This will help you prepare yourself for the future and get more comfortable making significant purchases. In this chapter, we will discuss the significance of planning and saving for substantial future expenditures. I'll be guiding you with the necessary insights and tools so that dreams like buying a car or funding your education become much more achievable.

THE ROAD TO YOUR FIRST CAR

After the COVID-19 pandemic, the significance of having personal transportation has increased phenomenally. When I was a teenager, many of my friends didn't learn to drive until they went to college, but that's no longer a feasible option for you. Moreover, being able to drive means you can finally stop depending on your parents to drop you everywhere. Learning to drive is the first step toward adulting, and you should start practicing with your mom or dad and then at a driving school as early as possible so that by the time you are eligible for a license, you are fully prepared.

Most teens start by driving their parents' cars, so don't shame yourself if you're also one of them. While it is perfectly fine to start with your parent's car, you need to start making plans to buy your own, too. Purchasing your first car is one of the most exciting things to happen in your life when you're a young adult. Still, it also comes with a set of expectations and responsibilities. To make the car-buying process smoother for you and your parents, here are some important tips that you need to follow:

- Before buying a car, you need to set clear expectations about handling the vehicle and meeting the necessary expenses. It would be best if you had a conversation with your parents about car management and how you will be meeting the associated costs. It is okay to ask for help; in fact, I recommend that you talk to them to avoid any disappointment. For instance, talk about how the gas and car maintenance costs will be shared and who will pay for insurance. Your parents might bear a bigger part of the costs, and that is perfectly fine. This will also help you put things in perspective and budget accordingly.

- Even if you have learned to drive from your parents or older siblings, investing in driving school is a good idea. Your driving skills will improve over time, but you should be aware of the rules of the road before you actually start driving around. I know it sounds a bit extra, but trust me, you'll thank yourself for taking the class after you see all the irresponsible driving everywhere. (Spoken like an adult, I know!)

- Once you've taken care of the technical aspects, you need to sit with your parents and set a car-buying budget. At this point, it is important to remember that your parents are trying their best to get you the car you want. Still, they also have many financial commitments they need to take care of. Try to use a portion of your savings and then have a conversation with your parents about how much they can afford. It might even be worth considering buying a used car because the price and associated insurance costs are significantly lower.

- If you opt for a used car, check its model year before buying to ensure the safety features are updated. I'm not saying you need the Batmobile, but you'll need a safe and stable vehicle, irrespective of how much you are using it. You can visit the National Highway Traffic Safety Administration website for more teen-friendly features to add to your car. You should also look for a fuel-efficient vehicle because gas costs can quickly add up, especially if you are frequently using the car for school and other purposes.
- Shop around once you have made your decision regarding a new or used car. It might not be possible for your parents to make a full payment for the car, and you might need to opt for an auto loan. Try to put a decent amount down to cover a portion of the cost, and you can take out a loan for the rest. There are plenty of financing options, even for teen drivers, so getting a loan isn't going to be hard, but there are certain things that you need to consider. First, try to keep the loan term limited to a maximum of 60 months because you should be able to repay it as soon as possible.

Getting your own car can eventually bring freedom, responsibility, and a sense of adulting that many teens desire. I had my license within two months after I turned 16, which was the legal driving age in my state. I started with my dad's car, and to use it, I had to drive my mother to work, then my father, and pick up both of them when they got out of work. Although it sounds like a lot of work, I loved it because I enjoyed my freedom. The point I'm trying to make here is this: Don't let social media fool you into thinking that you are missing out if you don't have a shiny new car that you exclusively use. There's a lot of honor in hard work and doing things in your own time. The sooner you understand that the more at peace you'll be with yourself.

COLLEGE FUNDS: START SMALL, THINK BIG

Even if you're a freshman in high school now, it's probably not too early to start thinking about college. I'm not saying you have to have everything figured out right now. Still, a college education is pretty expensive, and extensive financial arrangements would have to be made before you can start. In the 21st century, the average cost of a college education has more than doubled, with a growth rate of 2% per annum in the last decade (Hanson, 2023).

Before we talk further about saving for college, let's understand what makes the whole thing so expensive. Most students like to move out of their homes to a different state to pursue a higher education, which means there will be separate living costs that include rent, utility bills, food, and gas bills for the car. Mind you, all these expenses are over and above your college admission fees, tuition fees, books, and other things directly associated with getting the degree. Suppose you're attending an average private, nonprofit university. In that case, you will be spending $55,840 each academic year, which comes to more than $200,000 in four years (Hanson, 2023). These amounts are clear indications that you'll need to start planning as soon as you can.

Financial Planning for College

When the time comes, the expenses associated with a college education often come as a surprise to both parents and children. To make sure that doesn't happen, you have to be aware of how much it's going to cost. If you're planning to move out, you already know about the expenses since we discussed them in the previous section. The costs are lower for in-state tuition, averaging $9,678, which means if you have good colleges in your state, it might make more financial sense to stay back.

It would help if you also considered looking at scholarships that might be available for you. There is a notion that only "good" students are eligible for them, but that is not entirely true. You can qualify for a scholarship on the grounds of financial assistance, too. There are even special programs available based on other factors, like the nature of your or your parent's workplace or if you have a military background. You can learn more about scholarships from your high school counselor or financial aid officer, federal and state agencies, community organizations, or your parents' workplace. The U.S. Department of Labor has a free scholarship research tool on its website, which is also worth checking out. Depending on how much you are eligible for, a scholarship can cover almost the entire cost of your education or a small part of it. Either way, it is worth exploring because you are at least getting some form of assistance. The money that you receive from scholarships can be transferred directly to your college or given to you as a check.

Even though scholarships can be incredibly helpful, you should only depend on them a little and start creating a college fund as soon as possible. Because of the high amount of money required, you would need to seek your parents' help. Ask them if they have created a college fund for you because many parents make systematic contributions toward their child's higher education. Your parents' workplace might also have financial aid systems that you can avail of. To do your part, you can dedicate a portion of your savings toward building a college fund. Fix an amount that you can save according to your current levels of income and the time left for you to go to college. For instance, if you still have two years, you can set a target to save around $3,000, provided you have a part-time job.

Affordable Alternatives to College

I am an ardent advocate for higher education, and for the longest time, I believed that a traditional four-year college degree was the only way to achieve that. But as I grew older, I encountered many highly successful people who never went to college. In fact, a large majority of the most prominent entrepreneurs in the world are drop-outs. Of course, I am not encouraging you to drop out. Still, I want to emphasize that there are many viable alternatives to a college education, especially if you're not very interested in academics. Why push yourself to do something you don't like when you can create a career out of the things you might be passionate about? Moreover, many students don't like the idea of spending hundreds of thousands of dollars on college education and prefer to focus more on skill development. If you've had similar thoughts, here are some affordable alternatives to college that you can explore:

- **Vocational Education and Apprenticeship**: Vocational and trade schools are excellent alternatives to traditional colleges, and they are significantly less expensive. You can also simultaneously enroll yourself in apprenticeship programs to enhance your skills and become an earning professional as early as possible. Vocational schools can help you get trained in things like the culinary arts, firefighting, hairdressing and cosmetics, law enforcement, STEM and technology, animal care and veterinary assistance, welding, and many other things (Kindall, 2022).
- **Community College**: Many students prefer the flexibility of community colleges over traditional four-year college programs. Apart from being less expensive, community colleges also help you get trained in vocational fields too. They are an excellent option for students who need to stay

closer to home and work during their college years. The credits earned in a community college course can also be transferred to a traditional college.

- **Online Self-Paced Courses**: Websites like Coursera and Udemy have revolutionized the world of online courses. You can learn literally anything you want in any subject, and these websites will match you with the perfect course according to your skill levels. Most of these courses are self-paced, which means you can learn at to your convenience. Many expert educators and prestigious institutions offer courses through these websites. While they are not free, they certainly won't cost you as much as a traditional college.
- **Joining the Military**: Serving your country can be a great way to learn life skills and meet new people. While this might seem like a less traditional option for most people, joining the military can broaden your mental horizons and help you gain a unique life perspective.
- **Starting Your Own Business**: If you have an entrepreneurial spirit within you, starting your own business after high school can be a great career option. If your parents have a business, you can start by helping them out or you can look for options that don't cost a lot of money at the beginning.

I know there's some taboo around starting work right after high school because most people don't like to imagine themselves working a 40-hour job at the age of 18 or 19. But trust me, if you think the idea of a job resonates with you, go ahead without any hesitation. The whole point of growing up is to be able to do things that make you happy and gain control of your life. If a job does that for you, then it doesn't matter what anyone else says. Moreover, just because you're taking a job now doesn't mean you can't go back to school later on. If you can work for a few years and save up a decent amount of money, you can return to school without having to bear the burden of a huge educational loan.

INVESTING IN YOUR DREAMS

By now, we've talked extensively about budgets and why you need to be mindful while planning for your expenses. There has been a constant emphasis on saving at least 20% of your income every month and making sure you're not making impulse purchases. After all, delayed gratification is the best way to save up for big-ticket expenses like a car or college education. But amid all that, make sure you're also setting aside time and money to invest in your dreams and hobbies.

When we talk about "investments," the discussion is automatically shifted toward financial instruments like stocks and bonds or other assets like real estate or commodities. However, that is not all. As a young adult, you should also invest in things that will educate and enrich you. Take that course you're interested in and plan to travel as much as you can because these are not expenses but experiences. Allocate a certain amount of money every month for your hobbies and interests to avoid breaking the bank while pursuing them.

The best part of budgeting and financial planning is that you don't have to sacrifice anything. You can practice any hobby and do anything you like without any problems because you are financially prepared for it. The fact that you get to do all of it comfortably is proof that you've taken baby steps toward achieving financial independence.

INTERACTIVE ELEMENT

Visual representation can be very powerful when you are trying to set goals and work toward them. You must have heard the concept of "having a vision," which essentially means having some goals that you wish to achieve. But unless you are actually seeing your-self in that position, it is hard to work toward those goals. This is where the concept of a vision board comes into the picture. The world is now talking a lot about "manifestation" and how magic can turn your dreams into reality. However, simply manifesting won't get the job done, and you'll need to combine it with hard work, perseverance, and visualization of your goals.

The best part of vision boards is that there are no rules on how you should make it. You simply have to follow a systematic approach. Here are some steps that you can follow:

- The first step is to decide how you are going to prepare the vision board. Making it in the form of a physical scrapbook can be a good idea, especially if you have an artsy side. But you can also make one on your computer using apps like Canva. I suggest you choose the latter for your first vision board because it will take less time. Suppose you really want to make it aesthetically pleasing. In that case, you can always make adjustments to it once you're done with the initial draft.
- Think about the time horizon within which you want to achieve your goals. Make sure it is a realistic timeframe because chances are, you might not be able to reach all your goals within a short span of a year or so. Five or ten years is a more realistic timeline.
- Set a timer of 15 to 20 minutes on your phone. Make sure to put your phone on flight mode during that time because

you need to use these 20 minutes to focus. You can use your cellphone for timing, but it should not interrupt what you are trying to achieve with the exercise. The reason why I ask you to do that is because you need to create a sense of urgency in your goal-setting process. Although it takes a while to understand what your actual goals are, you have to give yourself a small deadline to figure out the things you want to achieve first.

- Put on some inspirational music to get your groove going. If you're out of ideas, try playing "Elephant Music" on loop on Spotify or any other music streaming app you use. Trust me; you'll feel like you can conquer the world. Match the music with your timer for a dramatic effect.
- Try to think of all the things you want to achieve within your specified timeframe and make a virtual scrapbook. For instance, if your goals include buying your first car or laptop, going on a trip, and getting into your dream college, make sure to include images of all these things on the vision board. You should also add the estimated amount of money you will need to achieve each of these goals. Don't worry too much about aesthetics at this point; let it be messy because life isn't always aesthetic, and that is okay!
- Once the timer goes off, take a look at what you have created. If you have missed something, don't worry! You can always add it.

Creating a vision board will help you see what your goals look like and how you can turn them into reality.

As children, we like to depend on our parents for almost everything, but as we grow up, the dynamics change, and there is an urge to be more independent, especially when it comes to money.

However, things can get quite messy unless you know how to deal with your finances properly. Learning to handle and plan for big purchases gives you a different kind of confidence and opens doors for further financial exploration. Once you feel comfortable about these things, you'll realize that you also need to learn more about the world of banking. That is why, in the next chapter, we will discuss banks, how to open different types of accounts, what to look for while doing so, and how they can be instrumental in your journey toward achieving financial freedom.

UNLOCK THE POWER OF GENEROSITY

"It's just fun to help people."

— *MR. BEAST*

Money is a problem. Let me correct that sentence: Money is not a problem; our understanding and unwillingness to talk about it is. We discussed in the introduction how woefully lacking in financial literacy teaching the education system is, and as a society, it's something we don't feel it's "polite" to talk about. The result? Not many of us have a clue what to do when we get to adulthood.

Remember that statistic I gave you at the beginning of our journey together? Young Americans owe over $1 trillion. That's not because they've all been targeted by loan sharks – it's because of a lack of financial literacy skills.

That's not a problem you're going to have because you took it upon yourself to give yourself the education you weren't being offered, so if your heart started racing again when you read that statistic, relax. You're going to have everything you need to manage your money and make the most of what you have every step of the way.

I want as many young people as possible to have that opportunity – and I know you do too. Besides, as Mr. Beast said, it's just fun to help people. You get that warm glow of satisfaction that you can't really get anywhere else – and this is your chance to get it!

By leaving a review of this book on Amazon, you'll help other young people, who realize how important this is, find the guidance they're searching for.

Your review will make this information more visible to the people who are looking for much-needed financial help (and there are many!) – and with a bit of luck, together we can change the future for a whole generation of people.

Thank you so much for your help. Feels good, doesn't it?

Scan the QR code below to leave your review!

6

THE WORLD OF BANKING FOR TEENS

"The advantage of online banking is that you can pay bills super fast, and your account is automatically debited for each deposit and payment, making it easier to stay on track."

— SUZE ORMAN

Ever since I was a child, I hated going to the bank. My dad would sometimes drag me there, but it was always the worst experience. The people were mostly rude; it always took a long time to get anything done and to top it all, I was incredibly bored the entire time I was there. This hatred turned into intimidation as I grew older, and by the time I was an adult, I was scared of the bank. That's right. A guy getting a business degree was afraid of the bank. Just think of the irony here for a second! Anyway, when I was in college and was living alone, I had to visit the bank from time to time because, back then, money transfers were not as simple as they are today. Thankfully, the people at that bank were kind, which made things easier for me. Around the same time, I was learning about banking in my college classes, which gave me further confidence to approach banking operations without fear.

But things have become so much simpler with online and app-based banking operations. You can open an account, pay bills, deposit job checks, or have direct deposits, and send money—all without ever having to visit a physical bank. Despite the simplicity, there is still some intimidation and ignorance among young adults when it comes to banking. Many of them don't have accounts and don't see the point in the whole concept. In this chapter, we will discuss the significance of having a bank account, how you can open one easily, the differences between debit and credit, and the essentials of selecting your first credit card. All the information discussed here is foundational and tailored to your age group, so it doesn't seem too complex to you.

OPENING YOUR FIRST BANK ACCOUNT

You already know how I felt about banks when I was a teenager, so naturally, I stayed away from them for as long as I could. I had to open my first bank account when I was moving away from home for college. As much as I hated the whole thing, I realized how convenient it was once I got used to the basic banking operations.

As a teenager, you probably have access to your parents' bank accounts and credit cards, and you have the information saved on your shopping apps. Using their bank account is fine, but you need to have one of your own so you can learn the fundamentals of banking. In case I still need to make my case, let us explore some of the reasons why you should have your own bank account right from your teens.

- Let's face it, nobody is saving money in jars or envelopes anymore. The whole process of saving and investing money takes place digitally, and it would make no sense if you had to do it all through your parents' accounts. Unless you have your own bank account, you will never fully be in charge of your finances.

- When you open your own account, you will need to provide your contact information to the bank. This means every time you make a purchase, you'll receive a message on your phone, and you'll be able to see how much money you spent and how much is left. This process helps build a sense of accountability and allows you to plan accordingly.

- You will be eligible to get your own debit card along with your bank account, and most cards have different types of perks, like discounts and cashback on purchases.

- Having your own bank account and credit card account will help you build credit. This is going to be very helpful when you need to borrow money from banks for items like a car or anything else.

- Finally, let's face it—you'll have to learn banking at some point in your life, and that point will probably be the moment you step into college. So why wait till then when you can make your life a hundred times easier by getting acquainted with it now? The best part of opening your bank account now is that if you mess up or have any queries, you have your parents to help you out.

Steps to Open a Bank Account as a Teen

Opening a bank account has become pretty simple nowadays due to the prevalence of many online banks. You can open an account without even leaving your home. If you are not a legal adult, you'll need to open a joint account with a parent or any other adult, depending on the rules of the individual bank. Here is a step-by-step guide that you can follow to open your first bank account:

1. Decide on the bank where you want to open an account. It might be a good idea to choose a renowned bank like Chase or Schwab Bank because they usually have good customer service and a wide range of products available that you can choose from according to your requirements. It might also be a good idea to look for an online bank like Ally Bank, Varo, or Discover® Bank if you are sure that you don't want any in-person assistance. While deciding which bank to choose, check the minimum balance maintenance requirements, annual fees, availability of ATMs, and security levels offered. You don't have to go full Hercule Poirot on the bank, but ensure that it is a member of the Federal Deposit Insurance Corporation (FDIC). This would mean that the FDIC would insure the money in your account according to its prescribed limits. It is a good idea to check out the websites of all these banks because most of the information is available there.

2. After you've decided on the bank, gather all the necessary documents so you are on top of the procedural requirements. Whether you're visiting a physical branch or applying online, having all the documents ready will make things significantly easier. Some of the common things that are needed to open an account are your social security number, government-issued ID, and proof of address. There might be some other requirements as well, so if you are going to visit a physical branch to get your account opened, it might be a good idea to call them beforehand so you are prepared.

3. Instead of opening an account that everyone else seems to be opening, consult the customer care executive of your

bank and have them assist you in deciding which account would work best for your specific situation and goals. They are in a better position to evaluate and suggest the perfect product to you.

4. After your account has been opened, set up online banking so you can make transactions seamlessly. Take special care in setting up your credentials correctly. No matter how secure your bank's internal system is, it is ultimately up to you to keep your account safe. Use an online password generator like Avast to create a strong password with random keywords. (FYI: Your birthday or your name followed by "1234" is not a good password.)

Some Common Banking Jargon You Should Know

One of the major reasons why banking is intimidating is because of the prevalence of jargon. You might understand the basics of banking operations. Still, then someone throws a term like "overdraft" at you, and all of a sudden, you begin to feel stupid. Let's end that cycle once and for all! Here is a list of common banking jargon that is going to make your life a lot easier and help you feel more confident in the way you deal with banking operations:

- **Account Balance**: The amount of money in your account at any given point.
- **Annual Percentage Rate (APR)**: The annualized rate at which you are paying interest on a loan you have. Suppose your education loan carries an interest rate of 5%; then that is the APR.
- **Annual Percentage Yield (APY)**: The annualized rate at which you receive interest on your deposits. This is the percentage at which the bank pays interest to you on the money you have kept.

- **Automated Teller Machine (ATM)**: This is an encoded machine from where you can withdraw cash, check your balance, and make other transactions like repaying loans and transferring funds.
- **Check**: A written document that acknowledges the fact that you are paying a certain sum of money to the person to whom you are paying the check. If you write a check for $50 to a local charity, then you are instructing your bank to pay the charity $50 whenever they want to encash it.
- **Credit**: A credit entry on your bank account statement indicates money has been deposited into it.
- **Debit**: A debit entry on your bank account statement indicates money has been withdrawn from it.
- **Escrow**: While a transaction is ongoing between two parties, an escrow is created to protect both parties' financial interests. A third party holds an escrow, which is a financial instrument where the payer deposits money until the receiver fulfills all requirements. While buying a house, a buyer would deposit money into an escrow account, and it wouldn't be transferred to the seller until the seller fulfilled all the conditions of the purchase contract. This will ensure that the seller is actually meeting their end of the contract and that the buyer is protected from any fraud.
- **Mortgage**: A debt taken to purchase a home. Usually, the house being purchased is used as security for taking out the loan. This means that if you fail to repay the mortgage, the bank can seize your house.
- **Overdraft**: The bank can allow you to make a withdrawal even if you don't have enough money in your account, and this facility is called an overdraft. This might seem a bit weird, but an overdraft is basically a form of debt that the bank allows when your account balance is zero. You will

need to pay interest on the overdraft, and there is also a fee associated with the overdraft facility.

- **Stop Payment**: This is an instruction you can provide to your bank to stop payment on a check that you have already given to someone. This would stop them from encashing the check.
- **Wire Transfer**: This is a transfer of funds from your account to someone else's by a wired network like the Federal Reserve Wire Network.

This list is not exhaustive, but it will help you get started on your banking journey. As you get more comfortable with banking operations, you will feel more confident in dealing with the more complex concepts.

DEBIT VS. CREDIT CARDS: WHAT'S THE DIFFERENCE?

Debit and credit cards are the most commonly used financial instruments by young adults worldwide. But there needs to be more clarity regarding how they work and, more importantly, which one is better. Although we explained the concept of "debit" and "credit," let us now talk about what debit and credit cards entail.

A debit card is basically an alternative to a paper check. When you make a transaction with a debit card, the amount is immediately deducted from your bank account. This means you are spending money that you already have instead of creating any debt. A debit card is directly connected to your bank account and thereby enjoys a high level of security and fraud protection from your bank. There are usually no annual fees associated with debit cards, and you can also withdraw cash from ATMs. On the flip side, debit cards don't provide rewards like credit cards do and would not help you build credit. They are an excellent tool for staying on top of your budget and avoiding using cash while doing so.

On the other hand, a credit card is usually issued by a bank or a credit card company and indicates a line of credit or, more specifically, a debt. We already discussed how credit cards work in Chapter 1, so I will avoid repeating it. They have a ton of advantages in the form of rewards and cashback, and they also help you build a good credit history. But the biggest problem with credit cards is that you need to handle the expenses properly and make minimum payments every month to avoid drowning in debt even before you know it.

Situations Where One Might Be Preferable Over the Other

At a glance, it might seem like debit cards are a thousand times better than credit cards. Still, you'll need to consider all the associated factors before coming to a conclusion. Using a credit card prudently can help you with long-term financial management. If you repay the entire bill every month, then it is a great way to manage your money and build credit in the process. The only time it gets unmanageable is if you start making minimum payments or spending more than you can afford. Suppose you're trying to build a credit score to qualify for mortgages or other loans. In that case, using a credit card instead of a debit card is advisable. Debit cards are good when you are trying to control your spending or need easy access to cash. Moreover, many retail merchants impose a fee when you make the payment through credit cards, which is not the case for debit cards.

In this context, I would like to mention that you don't have to "choose" between debit and credit cards; it is a good idea to use them together. A debit card can be used for most of your daily expenses and can help you manage your spending mindfully. But as a young adult, you also need to consider the importance of building a good credit score, which is why you also need to regularly use a credit card. To make sure you are making a few transactions every month, use your credit card for a couple of your automatic subscriptions, like Netflix or Spotify. Look for specific reward points or cashback offers on your card and spend only on those platforms. For instance, if your card is giving you reward points for shopping at Target, then use the card there. Set a maximum of five to seven transactions that you will be doing every month on your credit card just to keep it running and active. For all the other transactions, you can use your debit card. If you can maintain this rule, you are less likely to fall into the trap of credit card debt.

TIPS FOR CHOOSING YOUR FIRST CREDIT CARD

For the longest time, parents were against allowing their teenage children to use credit cards. This was primarily because of the common belief that credit cards are inherently bad and that teenagers might misuse them. However, things have changed now, and most teens are encouraged to use credit cards for building credit and learning long-term financial management. Having said that, choosing a credit card can be pretty tricky, especially for teenagers, which is why I have listed a few important tips that you can follow:

- After comprehensive research, if you find a credit card that's "best in the market," then that one probably isn't for you. This is because the best credit cards are usually geared toward more experienced users, and you might not even qualify for them. You need to look for cards designed for students that have a smaller limit and can be obtained even with no or a very low credit score.

- It is a good idea to go for secured credit cards, where you can get access to a card after putting down a deposit. Your credit limit will depend on the amount of deposit, and these cards are usually much easier to obtain.
- The fees associated with every credit card are clearly mentioned on the respective websites. So make sure you are choosing a card with the minimum fees because it can add up quickly.
- Don't stress too much about the benefits your card is providing. You have to ensure that the benefits are actually useful to you. Even if a card has multiple reward and cashback options, if you won't be using most of them, that card is not useful for you.

This is not a warning, but your first credit card can make or break your credit score, so be sure to use it properly. Set reminders for your due dates every month so you can make the payments on time. You should also keep your credit card usage to around 30% of your total credit limit. So, if you have a limit of $500, then your monthly spending should not exceed $150. Delaying payments and maxing out your card can hurt your credit score. Moreover, it would be best if you made it a habit to pay your credit card bills in full every month. Even if you can't pay the full amount, pay more than the minimum because if you do that, you will pay a lot of interest for a very long time.

INTERACTIVE ELEMENT

Now that you are aware of the common banking jargon, let's play a fun puzzle and guess some of the terms based on the hints provided.

Hint 1: A loan you take to buy a house: _____

Hint 2: A machine from which you can withdraw money: _____

(Bonus Points if you can guess the full form!)

Hint 3: This indicates money coming into your account: _____

Hint 4: This feature allows you to make withdrawals even if you don't have any money in your bank account: _____

Understanding the basics of banking will take you a step closer to getting a grip on how online transactions actually work. While this might not seem like a big thing, it will be instrumental when you delve into the world of investments. In the next chapter, we will discuss investments for teens and how you can remove the fear associated with investing and start your journey with confidence.

7

INVESTING 101 FOR TEENS

"I'd rather regret the risks that didn't work out than the chances I didn't take at all."

— SIMONE BILES

I 've been a bit of a dreamer right from my childhood, and by the time I reached my teens, I wanted to achieve big things, pretty much like every other young adult. When I was 17, I aspired to become a millionaire by 30, and I worked really hard to get to that goal. I admit it was a somewhat aggressive target and not very realistic, but it inspired me to move ahead. This was the time when I started investing and realized how much potential your money can have if you put it in the right places. Right in my teens, I realized that I needed something more than just savings if I wanted to achieve all my goals.

I won't claim that I didn't make any mistakes when I started investing; I messed up plenty, but because I started early, I also got plenty of time to recover from them and earn even bigger profits. I learned from my mistakes and made smarter decisions. Like everything else, learning about investing is also much more accessible today, which is why, in this chapter, I will be walking you through the basics of stock markets and real estate investments so you can be aware of the inherent risks and rewards of investing. We will also talk about some important strategies so you can remove the fear associated with investing and keep your money safe.

A SIMPLE GUIDE TO STOCK MARKET BASICS

When it comes to investing, stock markets are always the first option that comes to mind. But the funny thing is that most people (both teens and adults) have no idea what stocks are or how the stock market works. While these topics are not what you'll call easy-peasy, I think you are smart enough to understand the basics of them.

Let's start with what stocks are and how they work. There's a common analogy that is used to describe stocks: they're similar to a slice of pizza. The company is compared to a pizza, while a stock is a slice. When you buy a stock, you are buying a slice of the whole pizza. This is undoubtedly a great way to understand stocks, but let's take the discussion up a notch. You need money or capital to start any business. The amount of money the corporation requires will depend on the scale of its operations, which means that the money you need to start a side hustle will be significantly less than what Amazon will need for its business needs. That is why these corporations turn to the general public to raise funds for their capital. Now, as an individual investor who has a limited amount of money to invest, how are you supposed to contribute to such gigantic companies? These businesses divide their capital into manageable pieces, known as stocks, which you can purchase as an individual investor. Each stock is priced reasonably, and when you own a stock in a company, you become its part-owner. Your ownership is limited to the amount of money you have invested. So, if you have bought three stocks of a company, each costing $50, then your ownership is limited to the extent of the $150 you have invested.

The best part about investing in stocks is that as the company grows, the value of the stock will also grow. As a result, your investment will increase in value over time, and you'll be able to reap great returns. For example, if the price of the stock you bought for $50 increases to $75 in five years, then you are making a 50% profit. But there is also an inherent risk associated with stock investments in the sense that if the company does not perform well, the value of your investment will also suffer.

So, a stock market is a place where such stocks are bought and sold. It is no longer a physical marketplace because all stock investments take place digitally today. Although it is called a "stock market," stocks are not the only things bought and sold there. Other financial instruments like derivatives (instruments that derive their value from other assets) and bonds are also transacted in the stock market. Bonds can also be a very good investment option, especially for beginners like you. A bond is a loan that the company takes from investors and is bound to repay on time, along with yearly interest. So, as an investor, if you purchase a bond, you will receive interest income every year, and your principal amount will also be repaid after a specified period. Bonds don't have the risk of underperforming as stocks do. Still, the reward is also fixed to the extent of specified interest income.

In this context, it is also important to understand the concept of a stock index. Once you know what stocks are, the next thing that comes to mind is the fluctuations related to stock markets. Even if you are not a big finance geek, you must have seen news articles mentioning things like "the market is going up" or "the markets have crashed." When you hear something like this, it usually refers to a representative part of the stock market, the stock index, which is essentially a group of stocks with something in common (Liberto, 2023). These can be stocks of the largest companies or companies belonging to the same industry. For example, the S&P 500 is an index that lists the 500 biggest companies in the United States.

So, How Do You Start Investing?

Once you know the basics about the stock market, the next obvious question is how you can start investing. Believe it or not, buying stocks is almost as easy as sending a reel to your friend on Instagram. Like everything else, investments also take place through apps. If you wish to buy stocks, bonds, or any financial instruments on the stock market, you can use a third party called a broker. You'll need to set up an online brokerage account with companies like Charles Schwab or Ameritrade. If you're not a legal adult, your parents will need to open a custodial account for you. Once you turn 18, the investments will automatically be transferred to your name.

There are plenty of options when it comes to online brokerage accounts, but I suggest you choose the ones that allow you to buy fractional shares of stocks. Let me explain what that means. Suppose the cost of one Amazon stock is more than $150, and that is a lot for you to spend on investments at once. If you can buy fractional shares of a stock, you can specify how much money you want to spend on that stock. For instance, you can buy a fractional share worth $50. Charles Schwab and Ameritrade both have this option, and it is a great way to start investing even if you have a limited amount of money.

RISKS, REWARDS, AND KEEPING IT SAFE

The biggest reason why investments seem scary to most people is because there is an inherent risk element involved in the process. Unlike savings accounts or bond investments, stock returns are directly linked to overall economic conditions. Multiple external factors, like economic reforms, political events, and other large-scale global incidents, can have an impact on company revenues, which can subsequently impact stock prices. That is why conducting comprehensive research before buying a stock is essential. Back in the day, I used the Wall Street Journal to look up the stock symbol and get the price, but now you can easily consult any online portal like Yahoo Finance or directly consult the website of NASDAQ, the Wall Street Journal, or Dow Jones Network. And let me tell you a secret: This research needs to continue as long as you are buying stocks because it is the only way to keep yourself updated about market trends. You should not simply jump on buying a stock just because you like the company.

Risk and Reward

Risk is an inherent part of any investment. Usually, the common notion is that the higher the risk involved in any investment, the greater the chances of big profits. Professional traders and investors use a risk/reward ratio to calculate the potential rewards of an investment for every dollar invested. For instance, a risk/reward ratio of 1/5 indicates that if you are willing to invest or risk $1 in an investment, you can make $5 from it. You can find out the risk profile of a stock on the brokerage platform that you choose.

Most platforms have comprehensive information about risks and past returns.

While talking about risks in investment, it is very important to understand how much risk you are comfortable taking. This is also known as your risk tolerance level or risk appetite. You can be a risk-lover or someone who loves the element of risk in investments; risk-neutral, which means you don't consider the risk factor while buying a new asset; or risk-averse, which means you don't like taking risks at all. I want to mention here that there is no proper risk appetite. You can feel anxious about your investments; there is nothing wrong with being scared to take risks. Risk appetite typically tends to change over time, so you don't need to worry about "losing out" on profits if you don't feel like taking big risks now. Let me give you an example of what this looks like in the real world. Recently, I wanted to buy a stock in cybersecurity, so I researched five companies I liked. I could have easily purchased stock on riskier investments and maybe made or lost more money because it was riskier. Still, I decided to buy Palo Alto Networks (PANW). I bought it around four months ago and have already made 50% because I chose to go with the best company and not a riskier investment with the hopes of a big reward.

Diversification Is the Key

While a certain amount of risk is unavoidable, you can reduce it to a great extent by diversifying your investment portfolio. Simply put, diversification means not putting all your eggs in one basket. While investing in the stock market, you should aim to buy stocks from different industries so that even if a specific sector is under-performing, others will help you make up for it. Apart from stocks, your portfolio should also contain bonds because they provide guaranteed returns irrespective of economic conditions. The main objective is to ensure that the overall value of your portfolio remains profitable, even if the individual stocks fluctuate a bit.

Diversification is also important because it gives you exposure to different kinds of financial instruments belonging to different sectors of the economy. Apart from risk mitigation, diversification also helps you benefit from the positive changes in different industries. For instance, if you already hold stocks in a few transport and pharma companies, you can invest in the renewable energy sector and technology to reap the benefits of the developments happening there.

When you're young, you are bound to make some mistakes, so don't beat yourself up if you choose a stock and then make a loss. Even the great investor Warren Buffet messed up when his company Berkshire Hathaway bought stocks of companies like Tesco and Energy Future Holdings Corporation and lost hundreds of millions of dollars (Chatterjee, 2023).

INTERACTIVE ELEMENT

While the basic concept of investing is simple enough, executing the process at your age can seem daunting. If you are a complete investing newbie, you are more likely to feel intimidated about the choice of investments and their associated risk levels. All of these feelings are normal, so don't worry! Start an investment diary where you can make a note of all the assets that you wish to invest in and how you plan to create a suitable plan for achieving your financial goals. Here is an easy format you can follow:

Financial Goals (Money You Wish to Earn by a Certain Age, Things You Want to Buy, etc.)	
Investments That Match Your Risk Appetite	
When Can You Start Buying Them?	
Opening an Investment Account (Write Down the Steps You'll Need to Follow, If You Need to Open the Account with Your Parents, etc.)	
How Much Money Can You Allocate Toward Investing Every Month?	
Check this Box When You Have Set Up Your Investment Account	
Check This Box When You Have Set Up a Systematic Investment Plan	

When you start investing, you'll be amazed to see your money growing, and soon enough, you'll be tempted to increase your investments to earn bigger returns. It is very liberating to see your money grow phenomenally over time, and it is also one of the biggest factors that will drive you to become financially independent. After all, the more money you can invest, the better your chances of making profits, right? That is why, in the next chapter, we will discuss how you can craft your path toward achieving financial independence and the exciting opportunities it brings.

8

FINANCIAL INDEPENDENCE—A TEEN'S GUIDE

> "Money is something that keeps you alive and healthy and just keeps you focused. It's the drive. It's the passion."
>
> — TRAVIS SCOTT

I've always been a firm believer in working hard and earning money, even if you are just a teenager. When I was in high school, I was already working full-time, about 26 hours on weekends, every holiday, and any hours I could after school. When I was in college, I was working a full-time job, two part-time jobs for the New York State Lottery, and going to college full-time. Until today, I pushed myself to the limit, and sometimes, my wife gets upset with me because I work 16 or more hours a day. Don't get me wrong, I am not pushing you to become a workaholic! But there's nothing sweeter than being compensated for your hard work and being able to do all the things you wanted.

When I was a young adult, working so many hours while being a student was not a very common phenomenon. Many of my friends were doing nothing apart from attending school, and nobody batted an eye about it. But now, when I open LinkedIn and see kids posting about their businesses and strategies, I feel proud of the millennials and Gen Zs. Not many adults will admit it, but you are better than us. I'm not just talking about the teens who have become billionaires but each and every kid out there. And I strongly feel that this potential can be further enhanced with a little guidance from a Gen X member like me.

In this chapter, I will talk about something that pretty much every adult always tells you—the significance of earning your own money. But it doesn't stop there; we will be going through options where you can convert your hobbies into income streams and build early foundations for financial freedom.

SIDE HUSTLES AND EARNING OPPORTUNITIES

A few decades ago, working two or more jobs was something most of my acquaintances would look down upon because, apparently, it was something "poor people did." Thankfully, over time, many of these strange beliefs have gone away. In fact, having multiple income sources is now considered to be one of the smartest decisions that you can make for your financial future. Working multiple full-time jobs might not be feasible for the apparent reason that you will need more time to commit to all of them. This is where the concept of a "side hustle" comes into the picture. In case you needed to learn what it means, a side hustle is any job or work (apart from your main source of income) that brings in extra money for you.

As a teenager, you might find searching for a side hustle daunting, especially when you barely have a "main" hustle. Don't worry!

You'll be surprised to know that there are multiple side hustles that teenagers can take up, and the best part is that most of them require little or no initial investment. Let us take a look at some of the most common options:

- **Restaurant/Café Jobs**: This is probably the most common side hustle that most teens start with. Getting a job at a local diner or restaurant is one of the easiest ways for a teen to begin working, primarily because it does not require a lot of experience or specialized skills to get started. You can wait tables or work at the counter (or both), depending on the size of the restaurant. If you are a big coffee lover and love experimenting with different flavors, you can try being a barista, too! Who knows? You might even bag a job at the local Starbucks because they do hire teens.
- **Jobs at the Supermarket**: Similar to restaurants or cafes, jobs at the supermarket are pretty easy to secure. You can be bagging groceries or managing a particular aisle of products. While this might seem like something other than the most attractive job, it can help you start earning money and learn some important skills. You also get to meet a wide variety of people, which is always an added advantage.
- **Tutoring Jobs**: If you often find yourself helping your friends at school with subjects they cannot seem to understand, you might have a knack for tutoring. You can start with small batches to see how things go, and if you're doing well, you can increase the number of people, too. Online tutoring is also a great idea and opens up a lot of opportunities where you won't even have to leave your home.

- **Babysitting**: This is one of the most traditional teenage jobs out there, and almost everyone has done it once in their life. If you are generally good with kids and they seem to listen to you, then babysitting can be a great side hustle. Good babysitters are in huge demand, especially because most couples are working nowadays, so if you're doing it correctly, your side hustle can pick up very quickly!

- **Dog Walking**: If you have a dog or love dogs in general (like me), then dog walking is a great side hustle. You get to meet new dogs, earn money, and even get a lot of exercise in the process. It is a win-win for everyone. But make sure you are actually comfortable with the dog with whom you are supposed to be walking. It might be a good idea to start with smaller and calmer dogs who are easier to handle.

- **Tech-Related Jobs**: After the COVID-19 pandemic, most restaurants and cafes are trying to build an online menu so customers can place orders from it. If you have experience with app design and other technical things, you can look for these types of jobs. You can also provide tech tutoring to older people because we all know they need it!

- **Online Surveys**: Completing online surveys can be a good way to make additional money in your spare time, but I'm not going to put a lot of emphasis on this one because it can easily get you hooked.

- **Freelance Writing and Designing**: If you're good with words or paint, becoming a freelance writer or graphic designer is a very good option. Check out the available opportunities online and apply accordingly. Once you are a legal adult, you should also consider creating a profile on platforms like Upwork and Fiverr, where you can get access to a huge range of jobs.

- **Home and Landscape Maintenance Jobs**: Jobs like lawn mowing, cleaning houses, pools, or shoveling snow are great options to earn a bit of extra cash in your spare time. You never know; you might have a real talent for these kinds of things and end up starting your own contractor service business soon!

TURNING PASSION INTO PROFIT

Although the whole concept of side hustles revolves around earning more money, I strongly recommend exploring something you're really passionate about and then converting it into a profitable venture. Many companies that are huge corporations today, like The Walt Disney Company, Amazon, and Three Bird Nest, started as passion projects.

I know it probably sounds too good to be true at this point, but if you put a bit of well-directed effort into the process, you will be able to find out how to monetize your passion. Let's see what that is going to look like:

- The first step here is some good old self-reflection to find out what skills and passions you have. Close your eyes, concentrate, and try to think of all the things you really like to do and all the things you are really good at. Now try to find some common ground between these two lists. For instance, if you love dogs and are also very good at handling them, then dog walking or pet sitting can be a great side hustle for you. But to really make a profitable venture out of it, you'll need to expand on this concept further.

- You would need to discover a niche within your desired skills to make sure you are doing something really unique and adding value to your target audience.
- Speaking of a target audience, you will have to conduct research to ensure that the product or service that you're willing to offer has a legitimate demand. If people don't want it, there is no point in trying to sell it!
- Advertise and advocate for yourself. Social media has made it very easy for everyone to reach a huge global audience. So, all you have to do is post regularly about your product or service and create a brand for yourself.

It's not going to be a linear process, but it's worth a shot, especially if you feel like you can make something profitable out of your skills. In this context, I would like to mention something very important. It is not mandatory for you to try to monetize all your hobbies. So, if you like to curl up on your bed and read in your free time, you don't have to think of ways to turn it into a business if you don't want to. Social media can make it very hard to have a private life because everyone always wants to post every single moment and the details of their actions.

The Concept of Passive Income

The power of pursuing your passion is that if you do it correctly, you can build a business that can earn you a lot of money even if you are not actively working on it anymore. Before discussing further how you can do that, let me share a small story about Mikaila Ulmer, the founder of the much-talked-about Me & The Bees Classic Lemonade. Mikaila was only four when she came up with the idea of this lemonade from a book gifted to her by her great-grandmother. What started as a lemonade stand in front of her house has now grown into a business that makes more than seven figures in sales (Yates, 2022). At 20, even if Mikaila does not actively manage her own business on a daily basis, she has built a very comfortable income stream for herself and her family.

This is what passive income looks like. It is income that you are earning without active participation in the earning process from assets that you have already acquired. This can be profits from a business, earnings from your investments, or anything else. Your business venture does not have to resemble Mikaila's or anyone else's. You can look for inspiration, but you also need to have your own ideas and find a niche that resonates with you. Maybe you are a big murder mystery fan, and you can start a "Bookstagram" where you talk about your latest reads and provide recommendations. Becoming an influencer can be very profitable because most of us spend the majority of our day on our phones and on social media. Irrespective of the path you choose, remember that it won't be very easy, but it's definitely going to be worth it!

While discussing side hustles and building a business in your teens, I would like to discuss something very important. It is incredible to see young kids create multi-billion-dollar businesses from their YouTube channels or the products they make. While you should definitely take inspiration from them, don't let it influence you too much. If you are in high school and have a part-time job, and you feel that a side hustle is going to be a lot for you to manage, then wait to jump into it. Take time to plan and recognize your talents because that is also a process. Don't let the trends deviate you from your education or your current priorities, and trust yourself to make the right decision.

INTERACTIVE ELEMENT

The best part about being a teenager now is that if you decide to take up a side hustle, you have a billion options to choose from.

Even though that can seem convenient for some, it can also be quite overwhelming to select a suitable side hustle for yourself and build a sustainable income stream from it. That is why it is good to have a side hustle blueprint that lists some top options based on your interests and other important details to help you get started. Here is a simple format that you can follow:

Side Hustle Blueprint				
Skill Sets/ Interest Areas	Potential Related Side Hustles	Market Research	Startup Costs	Potential Challenges

Conduct comprehensive research on the areas that you can explore based on your hobbies and related skill sets. This kind of format will help you plan out potential side hustles in a structured manner.

Starting a side hustle and getting a part-time job is the best decision that you can make for yourself. No matter what others say, there is nothing wrong with earning money at a young age as long as you know how to manage that money properly. In the next (and final) chapter, we will discuss some advanced, tailor-made financial strategies that will help you manage and grow your money more efficiently.

9

TAKING CHARGE OF YOUR FINANCIAL FUTURE

"The first rule of personal finance is that it's not personal and it's not financial. It's about your ability to make 10 changes and not get too depressed over it."

— JAMES ALTUCHER

Can you believe we have already made it through eight chapters of financial wisdom? I am so proud of you for being with me for so long! The concept of financial literacy is vast. It needs to be cultivated continuously so that your knowledge stays relevant. You can grow your money management skills over time. Now that we have reached the final chapter, I want to talk about some advanced financial strategies and discuss the basics of some commonly mentioned concepts that will help you make better decisions in the future. We will also explore some wealth-building habits and why it is important to give back for a sustainable financial future.

ADVANCED SAVINGS STRATEGIES AND WEALTH-BUILDING HABITS

By now, you are already aware that savings and investments form the foundation of your personal finance journey. All your basic and advanced strategies revolve around maintaining a steady savings rate and starting a systematic investment plan so you can reap the benefits of compounding in the long run. In this context, it is important to note that everything depends on how well you prioritize your financial future. As mentioned before, saving should not be a residual activity but something you need to do as soon as you get paid or receive your allowance. There's a popular savings strategy that talks about "paying yourself first," which essentially means that as soon as you receive your weekly or monthly pay, you should contribute a certain percentage toward your savings accounts.

Use a high-yield savings account instead of a traditional one to make sure you're getting the most out of the money you're saving. You'll receive interest at a higher rate and can easily contribute to your savings without the risk of market fluctuations. Unlike a certificate of deposit, your money isn't locked in, and you can withdraw it any time you want without any penalties. Although there are some minimum requirements to open this account, it is worth it because of the many benefits.

Consistent Investing

No matter how much money you save, you have to invest a large portion of it so you can start earning phenomenal returns. Saving is simply setting your money aside, but investing is where the real magic happens. Even if you are keeping all your money in high-yield savings accounts, the interest income will be nowhere near the returns you can earn from investing in the stock market. If you feel intimidated to choose individual stocks, then you can opt for mutual funds or exchange-traded funds. Mutual funds are financial instruments that create a pool of funds from investors like us and use that fund to invest in different sectors of the economy. When you invest in a mutual fund, you are actually investing in several stocks, bonds, and other assets based on the allocation principles of the individual fund. This helps in creating a balanced portfolio and is very suitable for beginner investors like you. Exchange-traded funds, or ETFs, are similar to mutual funds and track the performance of a particular stock index (like the S&P 500), which means if you are investing in them, you are getting exposure to the entire index. Mutual funds and ETFs can be bought and sold using the same brokerage account that facilitates stock transactions.

Make it a habit to consistently invest even small amounts of money right from your teens. Automate the investing process so you don't have to worry about manually buying them every month. By the time you graduate from college, you will have created a small fortune for yourself.

Keeping Yourself Updated

From a very young age, I bought a copy of the Wall Street Journal every day so I could look up stock symbols to buy. Thankfully, you don't have to do that and can subscribe to the online versions. There are also a ton of helpful articles and blogs online that you can consult to keep yourself updated. Make sure to look at credible sources like Investopedia when you're trying to learn about some new financial instrument or market strategy. There are way too many opinion pieces out there, and I suggest you avoid them as your primary source of information. You can also consider taking a course or consulting a professional if you need further customized financial advice.

PROTECTING YOUR MONEY: BASIC KNOWLEDGE OF TAXES AND INSURANCE

Any discussion about personal finance is incomplete without the mention of taxes and insurance. These terms are thrown around quite frequently, but it is important to have a clear idea of what they mean and how they work so you can deal with them properly when the time comes.

You probably know it already, but taxes are money that you have to pay to the government on the money that you earn or when you buy things. I know it sounds a bit unfair that the government will take a part of your hard-earned money, but it is because the government needs to ensure the proper upkeep of the country and the community. Taxes are revenue to the government that they use for public expenses related to health services, infrastructural development, police, judicial services, etc.

If you are earning part-time, then you might be liable to pay taxes, and you'll need to check the threshold limit to see if you qualify for tax filing. If you are still a full-time student and staying at home, you can file your taxes jointly with your parents. At this point, I would ask you not to worry a lot about taxes but to understand that it is an unavoidable aspect of making and spending money. You should have a chat with your parents about how they file their taxes and find out if you need to speak with a financial consultant to know more.

Insurance is a contract where you pay money called a premium to the insurance company, and in return, you receive financial protection or get reimbursed for any losses incurred. Health insurance is an excellent example of a product where the insurance company will reimburse medical bills. Home and car insurance are also common, and any damages will be covered by your insurance provider. Most employers have insurance programs for their employees, and you may be covered by your parents' plans. Insurance is very important because we never know when an emergency will strike. It protects us from draining out our savings and ensures our needs are covered.

IMPORTANCE OF GIVING BACK

Since we're almost at the end of the book, I want to briefly discuss something usually not associated with financial management. In all our discussions about saving and investing money, we have constantly emphasized the importance of earning more money and building wealth for ourselves. But amid all of it, we also need to remember not to make our entire existence about money. That is why it is essential that you practice the act of giving back from a young age. Engaging yourself in community service can go a long way, both professionally and personally. Most students engage in social service because it adds credits while they're applying for college. Although there is nothing wrong with that, the act of giving back should not be for this reason only. Irrespective of the type of social service you are doing, it is bound to have a profound physical and mental impact on you. While volunteering at the local pet shelter or at a charity that works with disabled, underprivileged kids, you get to see a different side of the world. You develop a sense of responsibility and accountability that goes beyond taking care of yourself or managing your own stuff.

It is psychologically proven that taking some time out from your busy daily schedule for these activities makes you happier and more fulfilled as a person (Heldt, 2021). This will also have a direct impact on how you make your life decisions. For instance, you will feel the need to review unnecessary expenses, cut back, and be more mindful about your finances.

When you become aware of the bigger social issues, you are automatically inclined to make better choices. You can also follow these values in your financial management journey by exploring more ethical investments, like companies whose vision and mission match your personal ethics. This can also include investing in companies that treat their employees well and are conscious of the environment.

INTERACTIVE ELEMENT

Managing your finances is certainly a challenging task at any age, and it can be even more overwhelming when you are in your teens. To ensure you cultivate a positive money mindset and build accountability for your financial decisions, you can try journaling and noting down your thoughts surrounding money. Journaling can be a powerful tool to ground yourself and understand your feelings about anything. In case you are new to this, here are a few prompts to help you get started:

How do you feel when you have to buy something you need? Does the feeling change when you have to buy something you want?

Do you think you can talk about money openly in front of your parents and other elders? If not, can you take steps to change the situation?

How do you feel about saving money?

Does delayed gratification frustrate you at times? Note down a couple of instances when you did not wait and made an impulse purchase.

Do you inherently associate money with happiness?

How do you feel about investing and its benefits?

In all my years of dealing with investments and money, in general, I have learned that personal finance is not just about numbers and how much you are making. Understand values, set clear goals, and take actionable steps toward them. Whether it's your first paycheck, hundredth investment, or charitable act, each step you take shapes your financial story. Always remember to focus on the big picture while dealing with the "now" to precisely balance your short-term and long-term goals. I know it can be hard to imagine how the future will look, and frankly, you don't need to worry too much about what might or might not happen. The only thing to do now is to start making financial arrangements (in the form of savings and investments) so that you are prepared for what life throws at you. Don't just aim to make more money; try to build a life where you have growth, prosperity, and purpose. The rest will fall into place, and you'll discover what you were seeking was seeking you all along.

BE SOMEONE ELSE'S FINANCIAL HERO

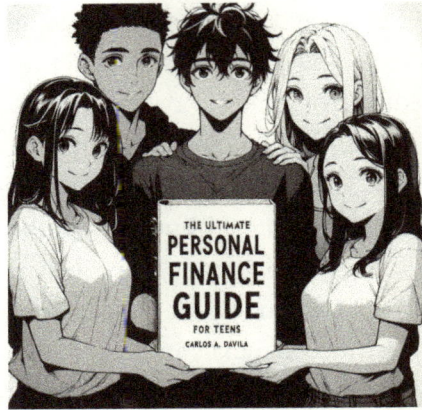

The ultimate goal may be *financial* independence, but there's no arguing that simply mastering financial literacy gives you an unrivaled level of independence. Why not offer that opportunity to someone else?

Simply by sharing your honest opinion of this book and a little about your own quest to acquire this knowledge, you'll show other young people exactly where they can find these essential skills.

LEAVE A REVIEW!

Thank you so much for your support. I wish you every success in the future.

Scan the QR code below to leave your review!

CONCLUSION

> "Succes is no accident. It is hard work, perseverance, learning, studying, sacrifice, and most of all, love of what you are doing or learning to do."
>
> — PELE

As a kid, my biggest problem was being too proud to ask for help. I always had a lot on my plate, and I wanted to show the world that I was a hero and could manage everything on my own. But obviously, I wasn't the hero I thought I was, and things would often get very clumsy and difficult. My parents were always there to support me, but every time I needed their help, I felt like I needed to do better. I couldn't wait to move out because I thought I would finally get the freedom to do everything on my own without my parents' support. However, strangely enough, my perspective started shifting once I moved out and went to college. I realized the importance of teamwork and support because I would often need to collaborate with my classmates on group projects, and our professors made sure everyone was doing their part. We also had to take turns cleaning the dorm rooms, which further highlighted the importance of mutual support. As I grew older and my circle expanded, I realized that there was no way to move ahead in life without asking for help. I got my stepson into investing when he got a job at 17, the same age I started investing. He moved from New York to Texas a few years ago to live with his girlfriend, and a few days ago, at 28 years old, they bought a house. I'm not going to take all the credit, but this had a lot to do with me mentoring him on investing and financial management in general. Even today, he always runs his investments through me, once again proving the fact that even if you are a fully functional adult (with a girlfriend, house, and the whole shebang), you can always ask for help.

Growing up is challenging. You have to worry about yourself and your loved ones, have a career, take care of your health, and deal with any curveballs that life throws at you. Throughout all of it, money and effectively managing it will play a significant role in your overall well-being. It gets even more challenging because most of us grow up thinking that talking about money is taboo and subsequently develop a negative money mindset. But you took a step to break that cycle, so give yourself a pat on the back.

The moment you start building a positive relationship with money, you will feel less intimidated talking about it and handling it properly. Some people take a lifetime to achieve financial independence, so if you feel like you're not making much progress, don't be too hard on yourself! Time is on your side, and the best thing you can do at this point is to start small and stay consistent. Follow a steady savings rate every month and start investing as early as possible. We've already discussed why starting early is great and how compounding can help you earn phenomenal returns over time. "Starting early" is going to look different for everyone, so don't beat yourself up for not having a 50% savings rate in your teens. You do what suits you and try to strive for a better savings rate in the future. You can start exploring some side hustles to make more money and subsequently increase your savings rate.

Get comfortable with banking operations and not just making online purchases. Use both debit and credit cards to clearly understand the difference between the two. No matter how many books and articles you read, the best way to learn about these things is by using them. Be extra careful with credit card spending, and remember to repay the entire amount every month so you don't end up with a lot of unnecessary debt.

Talk to your parents about investments and mention the fact that you are interested in getting started. If you still need to become a legal adult, they will need to open a custodial account for you. Do a lot of research before buying a stock. Don't jump into one just because "others are buying it" or because you have an affinity for the company. If it seems too risky for you, don't invest in it. You should not feel uncomfortable on your investing journey. Trust your gut and be true to yourself. Your concerns about risk are valid; don't let anyone convince you otherwise. It's always a good idea to discuss things with your friends, but if you feel it's turning into peer pressure, it might be time to stop those discussions immediately.

Being able to manage your finances is a process, and by finishing this book, you have just taken a huge step in that direction. The willingness to educate yourself is one of the biggest virtues you need to have throughout your life. Even if you end up getting a fancy finance degree, you'll still need to conduct extensive research each time you venture into a new investment opportunity.

I have said this before, and I'll say it again: Today's teens are way smarter and better equipped than we used to be at your age, and that is an awesome thing. You know more about many things already, and the easy access to knowledge at your fingertips makes it even easier. For the rest, you can always refer back to this book whenever you are stuck.

It's been an honor to be with you on this journey. I am confident that you have all the necessary skills to get started on a path toward financial independence. Trust yourself, and things will fall into place. Godspeed!

If you liked reading this book and feel it has added some value to your life, please consider leaving a review! It will help someone else struggling with the same issues discover this book.

10

BONUS: TAKING THE NEXT STEPS TO EMPOWER YOUR FINANCIAL JOURNEY

W OW! You've just navigated through the twists and turns of "The Ultimate Personal Finance Guide for Teens," and you're feeling equipped with all the know-how to manage your money like a pro. I am very proud of you, so I added this Bonus Section just for you. This section isn't just about ending with many tips and tricks; it's about starting a financial journey that's all yours.

Welcome to the "Next Steps: Empowering Your Financial Journey." This section is your launchpad into the real world, where budgets meet daily life, and saving isn't just a chapter title. It's about taking what you've learned and putting it into action, making choices today that set you up for an awesome tomorrow.

We're diving into the cool stuff that didn't fit neatly into the earlier chapters but is super important for shaping your financial future. Think of it as the bonus level in a game where you can apply all the skills you've learned to conquer new challenges.

From crafting daily habits that big-time money savers swear by to exploring ways to give back and build a network that boosts your journey, this section is about adding depth to your financial toolkit. It's not just about counting pennies; it's about making your money reflect who you are and what you value.

So, get ready to explore, engage, and empower yourself. Your financial journey is just beginning, and this section is here to make sure you start on the right foot with a spring in your step and a clear path ahead. Let's dive in!

THE TEN MOST COMMON TRAPS TO SAVING MONEY

When you're a teenager trying to save money, it's easy to run into a few common traps that can slow you down. Avoid these traps and stay focused on the big goal: Financial Freedom! Here's what to watch out for and how to stay on track:

1. **No Clear Goals**: Saving is easier when you have a target. Knowing what you're saving for can keep you motivated, whether it's for a new game, a car, or college. You can start a journal, mentioned in the chapters above, and clearly write down what each of your goals are.
2. **Buying on a Whim**: Ever bought something just because it looked cool at the moment but then regretted it? Those impulse buys can really eat into your savings. Take some time to think about the purchase you are about to make. I suggest sleeping on it and waiting 24 hours. Ask yourself if this is a need.
3. **Small Stuff Adds Up**: That daily snack or the app subscription might not seem like much, but over time, they can take a big chunk of your savings. Instead of having that

cup of joe at the coffee shop every day, have it once or twice a week and save the remaining money.

4. **Keeping up with Friends**: I get it; it's cool to fit in. No one wants to be an outcast, so if your friends are always buying the latest stuff, you might feel pressured to do the same. Remember, it's okay to march to the beat of your own drum, especially when it comes to spending money. After all, it's your money!

5. **Not Knowing the Basics**: Understanding money—like how saving works and its importance—can make a big difference. If you're not sure, it's time to start learning.

6. **Not Sticking to a Budget**: With a plan for your money, it's easier to keep track of where it's going. A simple budget can help you ensure there's always something left to save. A budget is one of the most important actions you can take as a teenager and even an adult. Start a budget ASAP, even if you have little money.

7. **Forgetting an Emergency Fund**: Life throws curveballs. If you don't have some money set aside for surprises, you might have to dip into your savings or ask others for help, setting you back on your goals. Along with starting a budget, an emergency fund is just as important.

8. **Thinking Small Savings Don't Count**: Even saving a little bit on a regular basis is better than not saving at all. Over time, those small amounts can grow, especially if you're earning compound interest. The apps mentioned in the section below, like Acorns, can help you save extra change that, over time, can add up.

9. **Counting on Parents**: It's great to have supportive parents, but relying on them to fix money mistakes can make it challenging to learn how to manage money on your own. Taking control of your money matters, and the experience

you gain will set you up for financial freedom in the future.

10. **Not Using Tools**: Many apps and accounts are designed to help you save more effectively. Please take advantage of using them to boost your savings game. The section "Seven Apps to Start Your Financial Journey" mentions these types of apps to get you started.

By looking for these traps and making smart choices, you can build up your savings, reach your financial goals faster, and set yourself on a path of future wealth.

SEVEN EASY STEPS TO KICKSTART A SAVINGS JOURNEY

Ready to start saving but need help figuring out where to begin? Check out these 7 easy steps to kick off your savings journey:

1. **Set Cool Goals**: What are you saving for? A new phone, your first car, or a concert ticket? Having a goal makes saving way more exciting and real.
2. **Track Your Cash**: Keep an eye on where your money's going. Use an app, or just jot it down. Knowing what you spend helps you find where you can save.
3. **Save First, Spend Later**: Whenever you get money, put some aside for your savings right away and forget about it. It adds up over time, even if it's just a tiny amount.
4. **Find Ways to Earn More**: Babysit, walk dogs, cut the neighbors' grass, shovel snow, or sell stuff you no longer need (such as good old clothes and video games). More money coming in means more you can save.

5. **Cut Back on Extras**: Love that daily smoothie? Try making it at home instead of buying it. Cutting back on small things can free up more money for your savings.
6. **Use Tech to Your Advantage**: Check out apps that help you save or manage your money better. They can make saving feel like a breeze.
7. **Celebrate Small Wins**: Saved enough for that video game or concert ticket? Celebrate! Make the purchase and enjoy it. It's important to reap the rewards of your hard work.

Start with these steps, and you'll see your savings grow before you know it. As you become used to saving, you'll want to do it more and more, resulting in your savings curve steepening more and more. Happy saving!

TEN ACTIONABLE STEPS TO START A SUCCESSFUL FINANCIAL JOURNEY

Starting your financial journey on the right foot is crucial. Here are 10 actionable steps to help you, as a teenager, begin with confidence and clarity:

1. **Educate Yourself**: Start by learning the basics of personal finance. Read books, follow financial blogs, or take online courses for teens. Knowledge is power, especially when it comes to money.
2. **Open a Savings Account**: If you haven't already, open a savings account in your name. It's a safe place to keep your money, and you'll earn interest over time. If you are too young to open one on your own, have a parent or guardian open one with you.

3. **Track Your Spending**: Use an app or a simple notebook to record your spending. This will help you see where your money goes and find ways to save.

4. **Create a Budget**: Based on your spending habits, make a budget. Allocate money for your needs, wants, and savings. Stick to it as closely as you can.

5. **Set Financial Goals**: Short-term goals could be saving for a new phone or concert tickets, while long-term goals might include college savings. Having goals helps you stay focused.

6. **Learn to Earn**: Look for ways to make money, like part-time jobs, freelancing, or starting a small online business. Earning your own money teaches you its value.

7. **Practice Smart Spending**: Before you buy, ask yourself if it's a need or a want. Look for deals, use coupons, and think twice about "in-the-moment" purchases.

8. **Start Investing**: Even a small amount of money can grow thanks to compound interest. Research simple investment options suitable for teens, like a Roth IRA if you have earned income. A Roth IRA is one of the best investment options out there.

9. **Build an Emergency Fund**: Save a little money each month for unexpected expenses. This fund will come in handy for things like car repairs or sudden school expenses.

10. **Give Back**: Whether it's time or money, giving back teaches you the value of community and helps you understand the impact of financial decisions beyond yourself.

Starting your financial journey with these steps will help you manage your money better now and set you up for more tremendous success and stability in the future.

SEVEN APPS THAT HELP START A SAVINGS JOURNEY

Here are some apps that can help you track your savings goals and celebrate your wins, making saving money more fun, easy, and rewarding:

1. **Mint**: This app is great for budgeting and tracking your spending. You can set specific savings goals and monitor your progress towards them.
2. **YNAB (You Need A Budget)**: YNAB is about giving every dollar a job, including your savings. It's super for setting and reaching specific financial goals.
3. **Acorns**: Acorns rounds up your purchases to the nearest dollar and invests the spare change. It's a fantastic way to save without noticing, and you can watch your savings grow over time.
4. **Digit**: Digit analyzes your spending habits and automatically moves money from your checking account to your Digit account when you can afford it, helping you save towards your goals without thinking about it.
5. **Qapital**: This app lets you set savings goals and create rules for saving. For example, you can set it to save a certain amount of money every time you hit a personal milestone or celebrate a win.
6. **Chime**: Chime is a banking app that has an automatic savings feature. It rounds up your purchases to the nearest dollar and transfers the difference into your savings account. Plus, you can set up a portion of your paycheck to go directly into savings every time you get paid.
7. **PocketGuard**: This app helps you keep track of all your money in one place and shows how much you can safely spend while saving towards your goals. It's excellent for

understanding your spending and finding areas to save more.

8. **Goodbudget**: Goodbudget is a great app for you to start getting smart with your money—it shows you how to budget and save, which are super important before you jump into investing. It's like learning to ride the waves before you surf the big ones, helping you get your money game on point for the more important financial moves ahead.

Each app offers unique features to help you manage your money, save effortlessly, and celebrate your financial achievements. Check them out and see which one aligns best with your savings style and goals, and get started!

SIX COMPOUND INTEREST ACCOUNTS TO FAST-TRACK YOUR FINANCIAL JOURNEY

Starting a compound interest account as a teenager is like planting a money tree that grows over time. The best reason? **Time is on your side.** When you start young, your money has more time to grow through compound interest, which means you earn interest not just on the money you put in but also on the interest that money earns. It's like a snowball rolling down a hill, getting bigger and bigger. This can turn small amounts saved early on into significant sums by the time you're ready for big life moments, like college or buying your first car. The earlier you start, the more your money works for you, making it one of the smartest financial moves you can make as a teenager.

When looking for savings accounts with compound interest, specially tailored for teenagers, it's important to consider youth-friendly accounts that offer low fees, easy accessibility, and educational resources. Here are some types of savings accounts that might be suitable for you:

1. **Youth Savings Accounts**: Many banks and credit unions offer savings accounts specifically designed for young people under 18. These accounts often have no or low minimum balance requirements and no monthly fees. They're a great way to start saving and earn compound interest.

2. **Custodial Accounts (UTMA/UGMA)**: A parent or guardian manages these accounts for a minor. They can be used for saving and investing and have compound interest advantages. Once the minor reaches a certain age (usually 18 or 21), they gain complete control over the account.

3. **Student Savings Accounts**: Some financial institutions offer savings accounts targeted at students, which typically provide benefits like no monthly fees, lower minimum balance requirements, and competitive interest rates.

4. **High-Yield Savings Accounts**: Available at both traditional banks and online financial institutions, these accounts offer higher interest rates than standard savings accounts, allowing your savings to grow faster through compound interest. However, they may have specific requirements like higher minimum balances or limited transactions.

5. **Online Savings Accounts**: Many online banks offer savings accounts with competitive interest rates due to lower overhead costs. These accounts often feature compound interest, no monthly maintenance fees, and no minimum balance requirements.

6. **Certificate of Deposit (CD)**: While not a traditional savings account, a CD is a time deposit with a fixed term (ranging from a few months to several years) that typically

offers higher interest rates. Your money earns compound interest but is locked in until the term ends, making it a good option for long-term savings goals. Keep in mind there is a penalty for early withdrawal.

When choosing a savings account, it's crucial to consider factors like the interest rate, how often interest is compounded (daily, monthly, quarterly, etc.), any fees associated with the account, minimum balance requirements, and the bank's reputation and accessibility. Remember, the goal is to find an account that helps your savings grow through compound interest while fitting your needs as a young saver.

SEVEN PASSIVE INCOME STREAMS

Creating passive income means finding ways to make money without having to work all the time. It does require initial research, time investment, and maybe a small money investment. Here are 7 passive income ideas for teenagers, explained in simple terms:

1. Selling Digital Products: This can be anything digital you create once and sell many times, like eBooks, photos, music, or digital art. You make it, post it online, and people buy it while you're relaxing, studying, or hanging out with friends.

a. Create something unique, like an eBook, digital artwork, or music.
b. Choose a platform to sell your product, like Etsy for artwork or Amazon for eBooks.
c. Set up your product listing with attractive descriptions and visuals.

2. YouTube Channel: If you love making videos, start a YouTube channel about something you're passionate about, like gaming, tutorials, or vlogs. You can earn money through ads, sponsorships, and merchandise once you get enough followers.

a. Decide on your channel's focus or theme based on what you love or are good at.
b. Create and upload high-quality videos consistently.
c. Promote your channel on social media and engage with your viewers to grow your audience.

3. Stock Photography: Love taking cool photos? You can sell them on stock photo websites. When people or companies buy your photos for their projects, you get paid, even if you're just taking pictures for fun.

a. Take high-quality, unique photos that have a potential market (think about what businesses or bloggers might need).
b. Sign up with stock photography websites like Shutterstock, Adobe Stock, Alamy, Getty Images, Etsy, and many more.
c. Upload your photos with good tags and descriptions to help them get found.

4. Dropshipping: This is where you sell products online without ever touching the inventory. You set up an online store, and when someone orders, the product is shipped directly from the supplier to the customer. You make money by marking up the price.

a. Research to find a profitable niche that interests you.
b. Create an online store using platforms like Shopify or WooCommerce.

c. Partner with suppliers offering dropship and list their products in your store.

5. Investing: If you have some savings, you can invest in stocks or bonds. The idea is to buy shares of companies or lend money (through bonds) and earn more over time through dividends (a share of the company's profits) or interest.

a. Consider online courses or financial literacy apps to understand the basics of investing.
b. Open a custodial account with the help of a parent or guardian if you're under 18.
c. Begin with small, low-risk investments to learn the ropes, like index funds or ETFs.

6. Print-on-Demand: This lets you put your designs on things like t-shirts, mugs, and phone cases without having to buy a bunch of inventory. When someone orders a product with your design, the company prints and ships it, and you get a sale cut.

a. Create original designs that would look good on merchandise.
b. Choose a print-on-demand service like Printful or Teespring and connect it to an online store.
c. Market your products on social media or your website to attract buyers.

7. Creating an App or Game: If you're into coding, you can create an app or a game and put it up on app stores. Every time someone downloads it or makes in-app purchases, you earn money.

a. Come up with a unique app or game idea that addresses a specific need or entertains.

b. Learn basic coding or use app-building platforms if you're not a coder (like MIT App Inventor for simple projects).
c. Publish your app or game on platforms like Google Play Store or Apple App Store.

Creating a passive income stream means setting up a way to make money even when you're busy with school or hobbies. As a teenager, you can start by choosing one of the seven ideas, doing some research, and planning how to begin. Remember to seek advice from parents, teachers, or friends who know something about your chosen area. Good luck with your exciting financial journey!

ELEVEN THINGS TO KNOW BEFORE FLASHING A CREDIT CARD

Before you start using a credit card, you should know some important things to avoid getting into trouble and make the most of it. Here's a simple guide:

1. **Credit Limit**: This is the maximum amount you can spend on your card. Imagine it's like a bucket; once it's full, you can't add more until you empty some out by paying it off.
2. **Interest Rates**: If you don't pay off your card each month, the bank charges you extra based on this rate. It's like borrowing a video game from a friend and having to give back more games the longer you keep it.
3. **Minimum Payments**: This is the smallest amount you must pay each month. Paying only the minimum makes it take longer and costs more to clear your debt because of interest.

4. **Due Dates**: Your bill must be paid by this date. Missing it is like being late to class; do it too often, and there are consequences, like extra fees or damage to your credit score.
5. **Credit Score**: This number shows how trustworthy you are with money. A good score can help you get loans for big things later, like a car or college. It's like a report card for your finances.
6. **Annual Fees**: Some cards charge you just for having them, even if you don't use them. It's like a club membership fee. Try to avoid credit cards that have an annual fee.
7. **Rewards and Benefits**: Some cards give you points, cashback, or perks like discounts. It's like getting a prize for using your card, but don't overspend just to get rewards. Just make sure these types of credit cards don't carry a big annual fee that's not refundable.
8. **Fraud Protection**: If someone steals your card info and buys stuff, you usually aren't responsible for paying for it, but you must report it quickly. It's like telling a teacher if someone takes something from your backpack.
9. **Overlimit Fees**: You could be charged extra if you spend more than your credit limit. It's like breaking a rule and having to pay a fine.
10. **Balance Transfers**: This lets you move what you owe from one card to another, often to get lower interest rates. It's like transferring to a different class to get a better grade. The downside? There is always a transaction fee of 3% or higher. If you don't pay off the balance by the date given, you will be charged the regular interest rate on the remaining balance.
11. **Cash Advances**: Taking cash from your credit card comes with high fees and interest rates. It's like buying snacks at

the movie theater; it's much more expensive than bringing your own. Try to avoid cash advances.

Remember, a credit card is a tool, not free money. Use it wisely to build good credit and avoid debt.

TEN EXCELLENT DAILY HABITS THE WEALTHIEST INDIVIDUALS SWEAR BY

> "You are who you surround yourself with. I know that's such a cliche quote, but it's true."
>
> — SELENA GOMEZ

Adopting positive daily habits can set you up for success, just like many wealthy individuals have discovered. Here are 10 excellent habits they swear by, explained:

1. **Early Rising**: Waking up early in the morning gives you a head start on the day. It's quiet, so you can think, plan your day, or do things without distractions.
2. **Planning & Goal Setting**: Taking time each day to plan your tasks and set short and long-term goals keeps you focused. Knowing what you're aiming for makes it easier to get there.
3. **Continuous Learning**: Reading, watching educational videos, or listening to podcasts can teach you new things and spark new ideas. Wealthy people always continue learning because it helps them grow and stay ahead.
4. **Networking**: Building relationships with people who inspire you or can teach you something is crucial. It's not

just about what you know but who you know that can open doors for you.

5. **Staying Fit**: Regular exercise keeps your body healthy and your mind sharp. It's not just about looking good; it's about feeling good and being able to tackle big challenges.

6. **Mindfulness or Meditation**: Taking time to clear your mind can reduce stress and improve focus. Even just a few minutes can make a big difference in how you handle what comes your way.

7. **Healthy Eating**: What you eat affects your energy levels and how well you can focus. Wealthy people often choose foods that keep them feeling good all day.

8. **Time Management**: Being smart about how you use your time means you get more done. This can involve saying no to things that aren't important so you can focus on what really matters.

9. **Financial Planning**: Keeping an eye on your money, budgeting, investing, and planning for the future ensures you're always moving toward your financial goals.

10. **Gratitude**: Taking time to appreciate what you have can make you happier and more positive. It's easy to always want more, but remembering what you're thankful for keeps you grounded.

These habits are non-negotiable for many successful people because they create a strong foundation for making good decisions, staying focused, and moving steadily toward their goals. Starting these habits now, even in small ways, can set you up for a successful future.

SIX REASONS WHY IT'S IMPORTANT TO GIVE BACK

"In a world where you can be anything, be kind."

— *TAYLOR SWIFT*

Giving back isn't just about doing good stuff for others; it's also a smart move for your future. Here's why:

1. **Feeling Awesome**: Have you ever helped a friend and felt really good about it? That's because doing good for others makes us feel great. It's like scoring the winning goal or nailing a test; it boosts your mood and self-esteem.
2. **Learning New Skills**: Volunteering or helping out in community projects can teach you things school might not, like organizing events or working in a team. It's like getting free lessons in cool stuff that can help you later in life.
3. **Meeting Important People**: When you're out there making a difference, you'll meet others who are doing the same, including people who've already succeeded in areas you're interested in. It's like expanding your squad with mentors and friends who can give you advice and support.
4. **Building Your Rep**: Being known as someone who gives back can open doors. Need a reference for a job or a college application? Those you've helped or worked with can vouch for you. It's like having a fan club that's also your support network.
5. **Understanding the World**: Giving back puts you in situations you might not usually experience, helping you see the world from different angles. This can make you

more creative and better at solving problems. It's like adding new tools to your toolbox.

6. **Making a Difference**: Every bit helps, whether cleaning up a local park, tutoring kids, or raising money for a good cause. It's like being part of a team where everyone's effort counts towards scoring the big goal.

So, how can you give back? Here are some ideas:

- Volunteer at local charities, shelters, or food banks.
- Offer to help neighbors with yard work or errands.
- Start a club at school focused on a cause you care about, like environmental cleanup or a food drive.
- Use your skills, like coding or art, to help non-profits or community groups.

Remember, giving back isn't just nice; it's also a smart strategy for growing, learning, and connecting with others who can help you on your journey. Plus, it just feels good. So, why not start now?

GLOSSARY

401(k): A special savings account for retirement purposes. It can be sponsored by your employer, and you can put part of your paycheck into this account before taxes are taken out. If an employer matches contributions, make sure to put in that match. For example, if your employer matches up to 2%, make sure you are putting in at least 2%. You should aim to max out the yearly Roth IRA contribution and put the remainder in a 401(k) account on top of the 2% you have already provided.

Account Balance: The amount of money in your account at any given point.

Annual Percentage Rate (APR): The annualized rate at which you are paying interest on a loan you have. Suppose your education loan carries an interest rate of 5%; then that is the APR.

Annual Percentage Yield (APY): The annualized rate at which you receive interest on your deposits. This is the percentage at which the bank pays interest to you on the money you have kept.

Assets: Things that you own, like money, stocks, a house, or a car. Assets should have a monetary value.

Automated Teller Machine (ATM): This is an encoded machine from where you can withdraw cash, check your balance, and make other transactions like repaying loans and transferring funds.

Bonds: A bond is a loan that the company takes from the investors and is bound to repay on time, along with yearly interest. If you purchase a bond, you will receive interest income every year, and your principal amount will also be repaid after a specified period.

Bonds don't have the risk of underperforming as stocks do, but the reward is also fixed to the extent of specified interest income.

Budget: A statement containing a list of your income and estimated and actual expenses that help you get insight into your current financial situation and plan for the future accordingly. It also helps you achieve your financial goals more efficiently.

Budget Deficit: A situation when you have spent more money than you have. It should be avoided at all costs, and you must aim to spend within your means.

Certificate of Deposit This is a savings instrument that pays interest at a specified rate for a specified period. The money would be blocked for the said period, and withdrawal would only be allowed after paying a penalty. This is a good option for building savings for a specified purpose.

Check: A written document that acknowledges the fact that you are paying a certain sum of money to the person to whom you are paying the check.

Checking Account: A bank account you use for everyday transactions, including withdrawals and deposits. The interest rates are minimal or nonexistent, so your money is not growing in this account. Instead of keeping a lot of money here, it should be moved into another investment, such as savings, meeting your emergency fund needs, ROTH IRA, a 401k, stocks, etc.

Compound Interest: Compound interest, or compounding, is a process where you earn interest on the money that you invested plus previous interest earned on that money. When your money is compounding, you earn interest on the principal and the accumulated interest that you have already earned.

Credit: An indication of money being deposited into your bank account.

Credit Card: A card issued by a credit card company or a bank that comes with a certain limit up to which you are allowed to spend on the card. When you make purchases on a credit card, you are essentially creating a debt that needs to be repaid within the next month. In case you are unable to do so, you will need to make a minimum payment, and the remaining balance will be carried forward to subsequent months, and you'll need to pay interest on it.

Credit Score: A number that shows your creditworthiness. If you have a good history of paying back your loans, your credit score will be higher, and your chances of getting a loan for such things as a car or mortgage will be better. A credit score is very important to maintain, and try to always have it above 700.

Debit: An indication of money being withdrawn from your bank.

Debit Card: A card connected directly to your bank account that helps you make online transactions easily. You can also withdraw cash from an ATM using a debit card. When you use a debit card for expenses, money is immediately deducted from your account.

Debt: This indicates the amount of money you owe to someone.

Emergency Fund: A specific sum of money that you should keep aside to meet unexpected expenses arising from medical emergencies, job loss, or any other situation that can prevent you from earning money.

Escrow: While a transaction is ongoing between two parties, an escrow is created to protect both parties' financial interests. An escrow, held by a third party, is a financial instrument where the payer deposits the money until all necessary conditions are met by the receiver.

Exchange-Traded Funds: They are similar to mutual funds and track the performance of a particular stock index (like the S&P 500), which means if you are investing in them, you are getting exposure to the entire index.

Individual Retirement Account (IRA): A personal savings account for when you retire, with special tax benefits. The most suitable IRA for teens is a Roth IRA, which can be funded from after-tax income. When you receive the money after retirement, it will be tax-free.

Inflation: An economic phenomenon where prices of goods and services keep rising over time. As a result, money loses its value, and you can buy less for the same amount of money. The best way to deal with it is to make sure your investments are giving you more than the inflation rate.

Insurance: A plan you pay for that helps cover costs if something bad happens, like a car accident or your house getting damaged. The most common types of insurance are home, car, and health.

Interest: The income that you receive on your investments or the additional payment that you need to make when you take out a loan. It is usually specified as a percentage.

Investments: Assets that you purchase with the hope of earning returns in the future. Examples include stocks, bonds, mutual funds, etc.

Liabilities: Money you owe to others, like loans, house payments, or credit card bills. It is important to pay on time, as it affects your credit score.

Loan: Money you borrow and have to pay back, usually with interest. Depending on the loan type, some will charge very high interest. Never use your credit card as a loan because credit card companies charge a ridiculous amount of interest.

Mutual Funds: They are financial instruments that create a pool of funds from investors like us and use that fund to invest in different sectors of the economy. When you invest in a mutual fund, you are actually investing in a number of stocks, bonds, and other assets based on the allocation principles of the individual fund. This helps in creating a balanced portfolio and is very suitable for beginner investors.

Mortgage: A debt taken to purchase a home. Usually, the house being purchased is used as security for taking out the loan. This means that if you fail to repay the mortgage, the bank can seize your house.

Needs: Things that are essential for your survival, like food, clothing, and shelter. However, based on your personal choices and lifestyle, other items can also become needs.

Net Worth: How much money and valuable things you have minus what you owe. For instance, the total value of all your assets, like a house, a car, investments, and money in savings accounts, minus the total value of all your liabilities.

Overdraft: A facility where your bank can allow you to make a withdrawal even if you don't have enough money in your account. An overdraft is basically a form of debt that the bank allows when your account balance is zero. You will need to pay interest on the overdraft, and there is also a fee associated with the overdraft facility.

Passive Income: It is income that you are earning without active participation in the earning process from assets that you have already acquired. This can be profits from a business, earnings from your investments, or anything else.

Real Estate: It refers to property investments, which can be in land, houses, or any other type of building.

Retirement: The period after which people stop working a full-time job. Usually, retirement is associated with old age, but nowadays, a lot of people retire at forty or forty-five, too.

Risk Appetite: The amount of risk a person can comfortably undertake while investing.

Savings: The amount of money that should be set aside from your monthly income so you can meet your financial goals and build a fund for yourself.

Savings Account: A bank account for saving money that you don't need right away, and it usually earns a little bit of extra money (interest) over time compared to a checking account.

Side Hustle: Any job or work (apart from your main source of income) that brings in extra money for you.

Stocks: The capital of large corporations is divided into small units called stocks that can be purchased by individual investors. The price of each stock is usually affordable, and they are a great long-term investment option.

Stock Index: It refers to a representative part of the stock market, which is essentially a group of stocks that have something in common (Liberto, 2023). These can be stocks of the largest companies or companies belonging to the same industry. For example, the S&P 500 is an index that lists the 500 biggest companies in the United States.

Stock Market: The virtual marketplace where stocks and other financial instruments are bought and sold.

Stop Payment: This is an instruction you can provide to your bank to stop payment on a check that you have already given to someone. This would stop them from encashing the check.

Taxes: Money that you have to pay to the government on the money that you are earning or when you buy things. Taxes are revenue to the government that they use for public expenses related to health services, infrastructural development, police, judicial services, etc.

Wants: These are items that are not essential for survival but improve our quality of life. Similar to needs, wants vary from person to person depending on their lifestyle and personal choices.

Wire Transfer: This is a transfer of funds from your account to someone else's by a wired network like the Federal Reserve Wire Network.

REFERENCES

Ackman, A. (2021, July 6). *Needs vs. wants: How to tell the difference.* Forrit Credit Union. https://www.forritcu.org/needs-vs-wants-how-to-tell-the-difference/

Adams, R. (2023, October 5). *30 best side hustles for teens [in-person + online, 2023].* Wealthup. https://wealthup.com/best-side-hustles-teens/

An essential guide to building an emergency fund. (n.d.). Consumer Financial Protection Bureau. https://www.consumerfinance.gov/an-essential-guide-to-building-an-emergency-fund/#:~:

Ashford, K. (2020, August 12). *What is compound interest?* Forbes Advisor. https://www.forbes.com/advisor/investing/compound-interest/

Atkinson, J. (2020, October 14). *The power of compound interest.* Penn Student Registration & Financial Services. https://srfs.upenn.edu/financial-wellness/blog/power-compound-interest

Ayoola, E. (2023, December 19). *The 7 best budget apps for 2021.* NerdWallet. https://www.nerdwallet.com/article/finance/best-budget-apps

Benefits of compound growth. (n.d.). Schwab Brokerage. https://www.schwabmoneywise.com/essentials/benefits-of-compound-growth#:~:text=Compound%20interest%20makes%20your%20money

Bennett, R. (2023, August 10). *Seven simple ways to build good money habits.* Bankrate. https://www.bankrate.com/banking/savings/ways-to-build-good-money-habits/

Bhutada, G. (2021, April 6). *Purchasing power of the U.S. dollar over time.* Visual Capitalist. https://www.visualcapitalist.com/purchasing-power-of-the-u-s-dollar-over-time/

Biles, S. (n.d.). I'd Rather Regret The Risks. Retrieved from https://themindsjournal.com/quotes/id-rather-regret-the-risks/

BrainyQuote. (n.d.). *Search results for 'financial future'.* Retrieved from https://www.brainyquote.com/search_results?q=financial+future&pg=4

Budgeting for teens: How to budget and tips for parents. (2023a, December 11). Mydoh. https://www.mydoh.ca/learn/money-101/money-basics/budgeting-101-a-guide-for-parents-and-teenagers/

Buying your first car: A guide for teens (and everyone else!). (2022, January 13). Drivers-Ed.com. https://driversed.com/trending/buying-your-first-car-a-guide-for-teens-and-everyone-else

Carosa, C. (2021, May 22). *True stories of children saving successfully.* Forbes. https://

www.forbes.com/sites/chriscarosa/2021/05/22/true-stories-of-children-saving-successfully/?sh=1623 9202854

Chatterjee, A. (2023, February 24). *Warren Buffett's 7 biggest investing mistakes: What can we learn?* ET Money Learn. https://www.etmoney.com/learn/personal-finance/warren-buffetts-7-biggest-investing-mistakes-what-can-we-learn/

Chen, J. (2023, May 2). *Exchange-Traded fund (ETF)*. Investopedia. https://www.investopedia.com/terms/e/etf.asp

Chime. (n.d.). 15 Quotes From Our Favorite Money-Saving Experts. Retrieved from https://www.chime.com/blog/15-quotes-from-our-favorite-money-saving-experts/

Cohen, I. S. (2017). *The benefits of delaying gratification*. Psychology Today. https://www.psychologytoday.com/us/blog/your-emotional-meter/201712/the-benefits-delaying-gratification

CoinNews Media Group LLC. (2019, May 10). *US inflation calculator*. US Inflation Calculator. https://www.usinflationcalculator.com/

Compound interest calculator. (n.d.). Investor.gov. https://www.investor.gov/financial-tools-calculators/calculators/compound-interest-calculator

Cussen, M. (2023, December 15). *What's the difference between credit cards and debit cards?* Investopedia. https://www.investopedia.com/articles/personal-finance/050214/credit-vs-debit-cards-which-better.asp

DiLallo, M. (2015, January 31). *Investment guide for teens and parents with teens*. The Motley Fool. https://www.fool.com/investing/how-to-invest/investing-for-teens/

Earley, B. (2021, March 24). *Stuck in a rut? Consider making a vision board*. Oprah Daily. https://www.oprahdaily.com/life/a29959841/how-to-make-a-vision-board/

Emergency funds explained for teens. (2023b, December 20). Mydoh. https://www.mydoh.ca/learn/money-101/building-credit/emergency-funds-explained-for-teens/#:~:text=An%20emergency%20fund%20is%20there

Emergency funds: How much should you save? (2023, February 2). Capital One. https://www.capitalone.com/learn-grow/money-management/how-to-build-and-use-emergency-funds/

Ethical investing. (n.d.). Corporate Finance Institute. https://corporatefinanceinstitute.com/resources/esg/ethical-investing/

Fairwinds. (n.d.). *How to tell the difference between your wants and needs*. FAIRWINDS Credit Union. https://www.fairwinds.org/articles/how-to-tell-the-difference-between-your-wants-and-needs

Fernando, J. (2023, May 18). *The power of compound interest: Calculations and examples*. Investopedia. https://www.investopedia.com/terms/c/compoundinterest.asp#toc-pros-and-cons-of-compounding

Financial literacy for teens: Spending wants vs needs. (2021, February 23). American century. https://www.americancentury.com/insights/financial-literacy-teens-spending-wants-needs/

Financial, A. (n.d.). *Money myths buster quiz.* Addition Financial. https://pages.additionfi.com/money-myths-quiz

Finding and applying for scholarships. Federal Student Aid. (2019, November 13). Federal Student Aid. https://studentaid.gov/understand-aid/types/scholarships

Five benefits of a teenager bank account with debit card. (n.d.). Central Willamette Credit Union. https://www.centralwcu.org/articles/5-benefits-teenager-bank-account-debit-card

Five teen entrepreneurs whose success stories wow and inspire. (2021, September 20) The Startup Squad. https://www.thestartupsquad.com/5-teen-entrepreneurs-whose-success-stories-wow-and-inspire/

Flynn, K. (n.d.). *5 reasons it pays to start saving for college early.* MEFA. https://www.mefa.org/blog/5-reasons-it-pays-to-start-saving-for-college-early

Four reasons why you need an emergency fund. (2017, May 8). Discover Bank - Banking Topics Blog. https://www.discover.com/online-banking/banking-topics/why-you-need-an-emergency-fund/

Frazier, L. (2020, October 6). *Helping your teen make smart spending decisions.* Getcopper. https://www.getcopper.com/post/helping-your-teen-make-smart-spending-decisions

Gillespie, P. (2015, December 24). *How 3 investors, all under 25, made money this year.* CNNMoney. https://money.cnn.com/2015/12/24/investing/new-investor-how-i-made-money-in-2015/

Glossary of banking terms and phrases. (2020, September 12). HelpWithMyBank.gov. https://www.helpwithmybank.gov/glossary/index-glossary.html

Gomez, S. (n.d.). "You are who you surround yourself with. I know that's such a cliche quote, but it's true." *In BrainyQuote. Retrieved from https://www.brainyquote.com/quotes/selena_gomez_595130*

Gorton, D. (2023, August 22). *How does money supply affect inflation?* Investopedia. https://www.investopedia.com/ask/answers/042015/how-does-money-supply-affect-inflation.asp#toc-how-money-supply-affects-inflation

Hanson, M. (2023, November 18). *Average cost of college [2020]: Yearly tuition + expenses.* EducationData. https://educationdata.org/average-cost-of-college

Hayes, A. (2023, May 3). *Risk/reward ratio: What it is, how stock investors use it.* Investopedia. https://www.investopedia.com/terms/r/riskrewardratio.asp#toc-what-does-the-riskreward-ratio-tell-you

Heldt, A. (2021, February 17). *The importance of community service in a teen's life.* The Bridge. https://thebridgeteencenter.org/news/the-importance-of-community-service-in-a-teens-life#:~:text=This%20helps%20them%20develop%20a

How to make good purchasing decisions. (n.d.). *PSECU.* https://www.psecu.com/learn/financial-tips-for-every-stage-in-life/2020/06/05/how-to-make-good-purchasing-decisions

Increasing importance of private transportation during the pandemic. (2020, December 9). Continental AG. https://www.continental.com/en/press/press-releases/mobility-study-private-transportation/

Investing risk and reward. (2024, January 5). Federated Hermes. https://www.federatedhermes.com/us/resources/resources-for/individual-investors/investing-101/investing-risk-and-reward.do?hint=page

Kagan, J. (2023a, April 20). *Insurance: Definition, how it works, and main types of policies.* Investopedia. https://www.investopedia.com/terms/i/insurance.asp

Kagan, J. (2023b, September 11). *How overdraft provides protection.* Investopedia. https://www.investopedia.com/terms/o/overdraft.asp

Keeping a spending Diary. (n.d.). The Royal College of Nursing. Retrieved January 1, 2024, from https://www.rcn.org.uk/Get-Help/Member-support-services/Financial-wellbeing/Spending-diary

Kindall, J. (2022, July 7). *Alternatives to college: 10 options for teens to consider.* Teen-Life. https://www.teenlife.com/blog/alternatives-to-college/

Kiyosaki, R. (n.d.). "In the simplest terms, inflation occurs when there is too money in the system." In *BrainyQuote.* Retrieved from https://www.brainyquote.com/quotes/robert_kiyosaki_627024

Lake, R. (2022, July 5). *Budgeting for teens: What you need to know.* The Balance. https://www.thebalancemoney.com/how-to-teach-your-teen-about-budgeting-4160105#toc-teach-your-teen-about-wants-and-needs

Lake, R. (2023, March 3). *Teens and income taxes.* Investopedia. https://www.investopedia.com/teens-and-income-taxes-7152618

Liberto, D. (2023, March 2). *Stock market for teens.* Investopedia. https://www.investopedia.com/stock-market-for-teens-7112213

Liodis, N. (2022, June 15). *The Importance of Diversification.* Investopedia. https://www.investopedia.com/investing/importance-diversification/#toc-how-many-stocks-you-should-have

Martin, A. (2023, February 9). *Seven tips for buying your teen's first car.* Bankrate. https://www.bankrate.com/loans/auto-loans/tips-for-buying-your-teens-first-car/

Mills, A. (2019, September 3). *Teen financial toolkit – Wants vs. needs.* Cypruscu. https://blog.cypruscu.com/teen-financial-toolkit-wants-vs.-needs

Minimalist Quotes. (n.d.). Drake Quote. Retrieved from https://minimalistquotes.com/drake-quote-18115/

Money math for teens: The emergency Fund. (n.d.) Finra Foundation. https://www.finrafoundation.org/sites/finrafoundation/files/the-emergency-fund.pdf

Musk, E. (n.d.). "To make an embarrassing admission, I like video games. That's what got me into software engineering when I was a kid. I wanted to make money so I could buy a better computer to play better video games - nothing like saving the world." In *BrainyQuote*. Retrieved from https://www.brainyquote.com/quotes/elon_musk_656024

Orman, S. (n.d.). "The advantage of online banking is that you can pay bills super fast, and your account is automatically debited for each deposit and payment, making it easier to stay on track." In *BrainyQuote*. Retrieved from https://www.brainyquote.com/quotes/suze_orman_465794

Paulus, N. (2022, February 16). *How to build a personal finance foundation for teens*. MoneyGeek. https://www.moneygeek.com/financial-planning/personal-finance-for-teens/

Pay yourself first: A smart saving strategy. (2023). Wells Fargo. https://www.wellsfargo.com/financial-education/basic-finances/manage-money/cashflow-savings/pay-yourself-first/

Perry, E. (2023, June 15). *5 steps to create a vision board that does its job*. Betterup. https://www.betterup.com/blog/how-to-create-vision-board

QuoteFancy. (n.d.). MrBeast Quotes. Retrieved from https://quotefancy.com/mrbeast-quotes

QuoteFancy. (n.d.). Jennifer Lawrence Quote. Retrieved from https://quotefancy.com/quote/1288680/Jennifer-Lawrence-I-was-raised-to-have-value-for-money-to-have-respect-for-money-even

Report: 1 in 5 U.S. teens lack basic financial literacy skills. (2017, May 24). NEFE. https://www.nefe.org/news/2017/05/report-1-in-5-u.s.-teens-lack-basic-finan cial-literacy-skills.aspx

Ross, J. A. (n.d.). *How to define "needs" vs. "wants" and teach our teens something about spending and saving in the process*. Parenting Horizons. https://www.parentinghorizons.com/node/299

Royal, J. (2023, December 1). *11 best investment apps in December 2023*. Bankrate. https://www.bankrate.com/investing/best-investment-apps/#best-investment-apps

Sabatier, G. (2022, February 15). *Thirteen best side hustles for teens to make legit money*. Millennial Money. https://millennialmoney.com/side-hustles-for-teens/

Scott, T. (n.d.). "Money is something that keeps you alive and healthy and just keeps you focused. It's the drive. It's the passion." In *BrainyQuote*. Retrieved from https://www.brainyquote.com/quotes/travis_scott_824145

Seven money management lessons for teens. (2022, April 13). Farm Bureau Financial Services. https://www.fbfs.com/learning-center/4-lessons-to-teach-teens-about-financial-responsibility

Shoen, A. (2022, August 12). *Want an easy kids budget for allowance? The 50-30-20 rule works!* My First Nest Egg. ht:ps://myfirstnestegg.com/articles/kids-budget-for-allowance/

Spector, N. (2023, July 28). *Sixteen best side hustles for teens to make money in 2023.* Yahoo Finance. https://finance.yahoo.com/news/10-best-side-gigs-teenager-210018988.html?guccounter=1

Swift, T. (n.d.). *"I'm very aware and very conscious of the path of chose in life, and very aware of the path I didn't choose." BrainyQuote.* https://www.brainyquote.com/quotes/taylor_swift_450956

Teaching teens financial responsibility. (n.d.). CalmWater. https://calmwaterfinancial.com/teaching-teens-financial-responsibility/

Tsosie, C. (2022, May 9). *11 things to know before getting your first credit card.* Nerd-Wallet. https://www.nerdwallet.com/article/credit-cards/things-to-know-first-credit-card

Ultimate guide: Copper's guide to budgeting (for teens). (n.d.). Getcopper. https://www.getcopper.com/guide/budgeting#:~:text=One%20common%20method%20is%20the

Waggoner, J. (2020, January 24). *Then and now: What things cost in the 1980s vs. today.* AARP. https://www.aarp.org/money/budgeting-saving/info-2020/1980s-vs-now.html

Waters, S. (2021, June 23). *Delayed gratification can change the way you live and work.* Betterup. https://www.betterup.com/blog/delayed-gratification

Webster, I. (n.d.). *$1 in 1913 → 2024 | Inflation Calculator.* Www.in2013dollars.com. https://www.in2013dollars.com/us/inflation/1913?amount=1

Welker, E. (2010, April 23). *Decision making/problem solving with teens.* Ohioline. https://ohioline.osu.edu/factsheet/HYG-5301

What is delayed gratification and why is it so important in life. (n.d.). Tony Robbins. https://www.tonyrobbins.com/achieve-lasting-weight-loss/delayed-gratification/#:~:text=Why%20is%20delayed%20gratification%20important

What's the Difference Between Credit & Debit Cards? (2023, January 4). Huntington National Bank. https://www.huntington.com/learn/checking-basics/difference-between-credit-debit#:~:text=What

Whiteside, E. (2023, October 10). *The 50/30/20 budget rule explained with examples.* Investopedia. https://www.investopedia.com/ask/answers/022916/what-502030-budget-rule.asp#toc-importance-of-savings

Why teens should open a bank account. (2023, August 18). Get Schooled. https://getschooled.com/article/5966-why-teens-should-open-a-bank-account/#:~:text=Having%20a%20bank%20account%20allows

Wilson, M. T. (2015, August 10). *Confusing wants and needs.* Intentional Hearts. Https://Intentionalhearts.com/. https://intentionalhearts.com/confusing-wants-and-needs/

Writer, S. (2014, December 22). *6 surprisingly common student money misconceptions.* The Columbus Dispatch. https://www.dispatch.com/story/news/2014/12/23/ 6-surprisingly-common-student-money/23374868007/

Yates, S. (2022, June 21). *How Mikaila Ulmer started Me & The Bees Lemonade at age four then later hit the seven-figure mark in sales.* AfroTech. https://afrotech.com/ 17-year-old-mikaila-ulmer-is-behind-this-multi-million-lemonade-company

Youth financial literacy: Why is it important? (2023, June 6). United Way NCA. https:// unitedwaynca.org/blog/financial-literacy-for-youth/#:~:text=Early%2Dadult- hood%20financial%20decisions%20can

.

www.ingramcontent.com/pod-product-compliance
Lightning Source LLC
Chambersburg PA
CBHW031418180326
41458CB00002B/431